D0535908

GREAT PEOPLE IN HISTORY

NOTORIOUS TYRANTS

GREAT PEOPLE IN HISTORY

NOTORIOUS TYRANTS

Nigel Cawthorne

ROSEN
PUBLISHING®

New York

Contents

This edition published in 2013 by:

The Rosen Publishing Group, Inc.
29 East 21st Street, New York, NY 10010

Copyright © 2013 Arcturus Publishing Limited

Library of Congress Cataloging-in-Publication Data

Cawthorne, Nigel, 1951-
  Notorious tyrants / Nigel Cawthorne.
     p. cm. -- (Great people in history)
  Includes bibliographical references and index.
  ISBN 978-1-4777-0406-6 (library binding)
1. Dictators--Biography--Juvenile literature. 2. Heads of state--
Biography--Juvenile literature. 3. Kings and rulers--Biography--
Juvenile literature. 4. World history--Juvenile literature.
I.
Title.
  D107.C38 2013
  321.9092'2--dc23
                                        2012032497

Manufactured in China

SL002557US

CPSIA Compliance Information: Batch W13YA: For further information, contact Rosen Publishing, New York, New York, at 1-800-237-9932

Sennacherib

**King of Assyria
died 681 BCE**

When Sennacherib succeeded his father Sargon II on the throne of Assyria in 704 BCE, the provinces of Babylonia and Palestine rebelled. Over the following years, Sennacherib led a number of brutal campaigns to retake them.

Chronology

704 BCE	Succeeds his father as king of Assyria.
703 BCE	Devastates the tribal areas of southern Babylon.
702 BCE	Moves against kingdoms in Zagros mountains.
701 BCE	Puts down uprising in Palestine; exacts large tribute from Jerusalem for lifting siege.
700 BCE	Planned invasion of Egypt foiled by mice.
691 BCE	Defeats Chaldeans and Elamites at Halule.
689 BCE	Razes Babylon.
681 BCE	Assassinated by sons in January, probably in Nineveh.

Below: *Sennacherib, in a war chariot, returns victorious from the wars at the head of his army.*

The Palestinian uprising had been backed by the Egyptians, but Sennacherib's planned punitive invasion of Egypt was halted when, according to Herodotus, a plague of mice ate the Assyrians' bowstrings and quivers.

When a Chaldean king took over Babylon in 691 BCE and used the city's wealth to buy the support of the neighboring Elamites, Sennacherib attacked, defeating a joint Chaldean–Elamite army at Halule. He suffered such heavy casualties in the process, however, that it took his army two years to recover.

Then in 689 BCE, Sennacherib returned to Babylon (then the center of world culture), attacked the city, and destroyed it. The destruction was so complete that it shocked the ancient world. Prisoners of war were used as forced labor to rebuild the city of Nineveh, Sennacherib's palace there, and a city wall 8 miles (13 kilometers) long.

Sennacherib was assassinated by his sons in January 681 BCE. His memory is preserved as the subject of a poem by Lord Byron.

Pheidon of Argos

It was Aristotle who named Pheidon a tyrant—the first tyrant of Greece. In fact, the word "tyrant" seems to have been brought into the Greek language just for him—Pheidon is said to have begun as a king (basileus) *and ended up as a tyrant* (tyrannos).

The hereditary king of Argos in the eastern Peloponnese, Pheidon built up an army of massed infantry, the like of which had only been seen before in Asia, never in Europe. In 669 BCE, he defeated the Lacedaemonians at Hysiae, bringing him into conflict with the Spartans, who considered themselves the traditional slayers of tyrants. Pheidon defeated them and went on to take Athens.

Chronology	
669 BCE	Defeats Spartan army: declares himself sole ruler of Athens.
668 BCE	Takes presidency of Olympic games.
***c.*660 BCE**	Killed in Corinthian civil war.

At the same time the city of Aegina, which had built up its naval strength, was at war with Athens, the traditional naval power in the Aegean. Pheidon had allied himself with Aegina but, when Athens fell, he took Aegina too. It is said that he struck the first silver coinage there. He also introduced a standard system of weights and measures and many Greek cities, including Athens, adopted the so-called Pheidonian measures.

In 668 BCE, he intervened at Olympia and supported the Pisatans in their bid to take control of the Games from the Elians. He also tried to annex Corinth, bringing him into conflict with Sparta once more. Sicyon, Samos, and Mitetus also seem to have fallen into his hands.

Pheidon had allied himself with Aegina but, when Athens fell, he took Aegina too.

Aristotle described Pheidon as a tyrant because he depended for his power on military might rather than consent. In Argos, power was concentrated in one man's hands, not spread among the aristocracy as it was in other Greek states.

Pheidon seems to have been killed in the civil war in Corinth, which produced that city-state's first tyrant. Other tyrants soon took power in Epidaurus, Megara, and Sicyon.

Herod the Great

Born in Palestine in 73 BCE, Herod was the son of Antipater, who was named procurator of Judaea in 47 BCE by Julius Caesar as a reward for supporting the winning side in the civil war. This gave the whole family Roman citizenship. Antipater made his sixteen-year-old son governor of Galilee, where Herod launched an unpopular campaign against local bandits.

The murder of Julius Caesar in 44 BCE plunged the Roman Empire back into civil war and left Antipater and his son Herod short of money. The taxes they imposed caused an insurrection in which Antipater was killed; Herod, with Roman help, put down the rebellion and killed his father's murderer.

Herod managed to convince Mark Antony that the eastern provinces had supported him against Cassius and Brutus and was rewarded by being appointed tetrarch of Galilee, while his older brother, Phasael, became tetrarch of Jerusalem.

An anti-Roman insurrection forced Herod to flee in 40 BCE, while Phasael committed suicide and Herod's father-in-law, Hyrcanus, the king of Judaea, was taken into captivity in Babylon by the Parthians. In Rome, Herod managed to secure the backing of the Senate and in 36 BCE he rode back into Palestine at the head of a Roman army, and besieged and captured Jerusalem. The enemy fled into the hills and found shelter in caves. Herod pursued them, slaughtering men, women, and children.

Herod persuaded the Parthians to release Hyrancus, but refused to give him back his throne. Instead Herod took the crown, using the presence of the old monarch to buttress his rule. He began an extensive building program and minted coins with his likeness on them.

Herod was almost undone through his support for Antony and Cleopatra in their struggle against Octavian, but he quickly changed sides when it became plain he was backing a loser. He sailed to Rhodes to meet Octavian, after executing Hyrancus so he could not take the throne in Herod's absence. In a brilliant speech, Herod boasted of his loyalty to Mark Antony, then pledged the same to the new ruler of Rome. His audacity paid off and Octavian confirmed him as king of Judaea, it being clear that Herod would be a useful ally if Octavian had to pursue Antony and Cleopatra into Egypt. When Octavian became the Emperor Augustus, he rewarded Herod by giving him jurisdiction over Jericho and Gaza.

Herod ruled unchallenged in Judaea for thirty-two years. He rebuilt Jerusalem after an earthquake in 31 BCE, built new fortresses to

Chronology

73 BCE	Born in southern Palestine.
47 BCE	Becomes Roman citizen.
41 BCE	Appointed tetrarch of Galilee by Mark Antony.
40 BCE	Flees to Rome where he is named king of Judaea.
38 BCE	Returns to Palestine at the head of a Roman army.
29 BCE	Murders wife Mariamme, her two sons, and all her family.
4 BCE	Massacre of the Innocents; Herod dies March or April in Jericho.

Herod's soldiers massacre the Innocents in this engraving by Gustav Doré.

hold his territory, and built a new port called Caesarea in honor of Augustus. The taxes he needed to raise to do this made him extremely unpopular. The old royal houses whom he had deposed opposed him and the Pharisees condemned him for repeated violations of Mosaic Law. He was seen as a puppet of Augustus, who had offended the Jews by ordering that the priest of the Temple make sacrifices twice a day for Rome and the Senate. The Jews also believed that Herod, a pagan, was violating their graves and stealing gold objects from the tomb of King David. To hold on to power, Herod employed mercenaries and a secret police force. He also married ten times for political reasons.

As time went by, Herod became increasingly mentally unstable. He murdered his second wife Mariamme, her two sons, and her entire family, fearing that they were plotting against him. He also killed his first-born son Antipater, leading Augustus to remark that it was preferable to be Herod's pig (*hus*) than his son (*huios*).

In 8 BCE, the monastery at Qumran, the home of the Essene sect, was destroyed by a fire thought to have been started by Herod: he also had a group of Jews burned alive for removing from the Temple a golden eagle, which they considered a graven image.

Toward the end of his reign, Jewish scholars announced that seventy-six generations had passed since the Creation. They believed that the Messiah would be born in the seventy-seventh generation. According to St Matthew's Gospel, Herod ordered the slaughter of all male infants after hearing that a child born in Bethlehem was being honored as the king of the Jews. However, this is the only source for the story.

After an unsuccessful attempt at suicide, Herod died in Jericho in 4 BCE. His kingdom was divided among his surviving sons.

Caligula

Born Gaius Julius Caesar Germanicus, Caligula was brought up in the military camps of his father Germanicus and got his nickname—which translates as "Little Boot"—after the army footwear he wore as a youth.

Caligula's father died in 19 CE, and his mother and two older brothers were executed by the Emperor Tiberius in political purges, but Caligula managed to ingratiate himself with Tiberius, living with him on Capri. Tiberius said of Caligula that "no one ever made a better slave or a worse master."

Caligula married the daughter of a nobleman in the hope that it would improve his chances of succeeding Tiberius. After losing his first wife in childbirth, however, Caligula seduced the wife of Naevius Sutorius Macro, commander of the Praetorian guard, even promising to marry her if he became emperor, while at the same time he wormed his way into Macro's favor. According to Suetonius, Caligula then poisoned Tiberius, intending to take the imperial ring from Tiberius's finger and thus seize power. When the poison did not immediately kill Tiberius, Caligula suffocated him with a pillow or strangled him, depending on which source one reads. A freeman who had seen what had happened and cried out a warning was later crucified, on Caligula's orders.

The population of Rome was not sorry to see the back of Tiberius, and Caligula was a popular figure, his father being remembered with affection and the slaughter of Caligula's family earning him popular sympathy. He was also the first direct descendant of Augustus to come to the throne, which did him no harm at all.

Although initially popular, largely because Tiberius was so hated, seven months after his accession Caligula fell ill and the fever seems to have affected his brain. After he recovered, he instigated a series of treason trials of his own. The following year, he put his adopted son Tiberius Gemellus to death without trial and forced his father-in-law Marcus Junius Silanus to commit suicide after accusing them of treason. Caligula began to fear the growing power of Naevius Sutorius Macro, the prefect of the Praetorian Guard who had helped him to power. After sending Macro out of Rome to Egypt, under the pretext of making him governor of the province, Caligula had him arrested and executed.

Later that year, Caligula's favorite sister, Drusilla, with whom Caligula had had an intensely close relationship since childhood, died. Caligula announced a season of public mourning, during which it was made a

Caligula as represented in this contemporary statue, unearthed at the Villa Albani in Rome.

capital offense to laugh, bathe, or dine with members of your own family. He minted coins in Drusilla's honor and even had her deified, although her divinity was later revoked.

After the mourning was over, he took time off from running the empire and spent lavishly on games, banquets, and public displays. He built a pontoon bridge 3 miles (5 km) long across the Bay of Naples and rode back and forth across for two days. He built vast galleys, villas, and country houses, regardless of expense. Guests at banquets would find gold molded into the shape of food on plates in front of them. He would dissolve valuable pearls in vinegar and drink down the mixture. Within six months he had squandered the vast fortune Tiberius had left.

To raise money, he started a fresh round of treason trials (those condemned of treason in Imperial Rome forfeited their property to the state). Caligula would name the amount he sought to raise at the start of each day's proceedings: in one particular afternoon he condemned as many as forty men to raise the desired figure, complaining afterward what a tiring day he had had. He revoked the Roman citizenship of many who had earned it and seized their estates. Others were forced to name him as their heir, then were sent poisoned sweetmeats. Caligula also personally sold off the public properties left over after the games. One senator who fell asleep at an auction awoke to discover that Caligula had taken his nods for bids and he was now the proud owner of thirteen gladiators at a hugely inflated price. Others were forced to buy things at prices they could not afford. Bankrupted, some committed suicide.

Caligula had men executed for little or no reason. Senators were executed secretly and he would continue summoning them as if they were still alive, only announcing some time later that they had committed suicide. His uncle Claudius, it is said, was spared only because he was considered a laughing stock. Criminals were fed to his lions, on the grounds that they were cheaper than butcher's meat. After an oratory competition, he forced the losers to erase their wax tablets with their tongues, on pain of death. However, the story that he made his horse a consul is probably without foundation, though one horse was given a house with furniture and servants, and the entire neighborhood was ordered to keep silent so that it could sleep undisturbed.

Caligula's behavior became increasingly disruptive to the smooth running of the city. He would close the granaries so that the people would go hungry, or scatter free tickets to the circus among crowds, causing stampedes where many people died. He put on contests between mangy beasts and people who were disabled or infirm.

Men of rank were branded or shut up in cages like wild animals. Caligula even bewailed the fact that his reign had not been marked by any great catastrophe, saying the rule of Augustus had been made famous by the loss of three legions under Publius Quinctilius Varus in the Teutoburg Forest.

In 39 CE, Caligula went to Germany, where he discovered a plot by the military commander Gaetulicus to kill him and replace him with Aemilius Lepidus, the widower of Drusilla and lover of Agrippina the Younger. The

Chronology

12 CE	Born August 31 at Antium, modern-day Anzio, Italy.
19 CE	Father dies.
33 CE	Mother and brothers executed.
37 CE	Murders Tiberius and usurps the throne.
38 CE	Executes legitimate heir and those who helped him to power.
39 CE	Executes brother-in-law; builds pontoon bridge across Bay of Naples.
40 CE	Plunders Gaul.
41 CE	Assassinated January 24 in Rome by the Praetorian guard and other high-ranking conspirators.

two men were executed and Agrippina and the youngest sister, Julia Livilla, were exiled.

The following year, Caligula invaded and plundered Gaul, and planned to invade Britain, even having triremes carried overland from Rome to cross the Channel. But when he reached the English Channel, he contented himself with ordering his men to collect seashells from the beach, which he called the spoils of the conquered ocean. Meanwhile, he rebuked the Senate, accusing them of indulging in revels, going to the theater, and living comfortably in their villas while he was risking his life in battle.

Before returning to Rome, he tried to slaughter his own legions, ordering them to assemble without their weapons. When they realized what was going on, he was forced to flee. Despite this, he entered Rome in triumph. To pay for the parade he imposed many new taxes, for example on food, lawsuits, the wages of porters, and marriage.

Caligula had pretensions to divinity and built temples and statues to himself. Statues of other noted Romans were destroyed and even those of Augustus moved. He even thought of destroying the poems of Homer, and he had Virgil's work banned from libraries. The certificates of deification of Julius Caesar and Augustus were old and out of date, he said. And he ordered his own statue to be placed in the Temple in Jerusalem so that the Jews could worship him, though the procurator of Judea procrastinated and the statue was not in place by the time of his death.

Criminals were fed to his lions, on the grounds that they were cheaper than butcher's meat.

His wife Caesonia plied him with drugs to improve his virility, which made him even more mentally unstable. He often wore women's clothing or dressed as a god with a blonde beard or as Venus or a triumphant general, wearing the breastplate of Alexander the Great which he had taken from his sarcophagus. He also caused a scandal, singing and dancing in public and appearing on stage with lowly actors.

Caligula was already in danger from the legions in Germany who had turned against him. Now he deliberately alienated those closest to him, threatening to kill them and himself if they thought he deserved death. Omens told of his forthcoming death and a performance of a play was staged, showing the murder of a king—in this case, Philip of Macedonia, Alexander the Great's father.

On January 24, 41 CE, Caligula attended the Palatine Games, where he was stabbed at least thirty times by the tribune of the Praetorian guard and other high-ranking conspirators. As he lay writhing on the ground he was despatched, it is said, with a sword thrust through his groin. His wife Caesonia was stabbed to death by a centurion and his daughter was brutally murdered.

Caligula was just twenty-nine and had ruled for less than four years when he was assassinated. His body was taken secretly to the garden of the Lamian family, partially burned in a hastily constructed funeral pyre, then buried. When his sisters returned from exile, they had it dug up and cremated properly, and the ashes placed in the family tomb. His uncle Claudius, whom Caligula had spared as a laughing stock, succeeded him as emperor.

Agrippina

Julia Agrippina, also known as Agrippina Minor or Agrippina the Younger, combined beauty with ruthless ambition and a propensity for violence. She took advantage of her closeness to powerful males to wield her own influence.

"Empress" of Rome 15–59 CE

Agrippina the Younger was the great-granddaughter of the Roman Emperor Augustus and sister of the Emperor Caligula. In 39 CE, Caligula exiled her for conspiring against him, but he allowed her to return to Rome in 41 CE. In 49 CE, Agrippina saw her main chance, and seized it. She poisoned her second husband, Passienus Crispus, and then married her uncle, the Emperor Claudius, by then an old and feeble man, and effectively took control.

Agrippina soon bullied Claudius into adopting her son, Nero, and strengthened Nero's position further by marrying him to Claudius's daughter Octavia. Meanwhile, Agrippina poisoned all potential rivals. It is very likely that she also murdered Claudius, who died in 54 CE after eating poisoned mushrooms, along with his son and heir, Britannicus. Nero became emperor, but Agrippina held on to power as regent, taking the title AVGVSTA, meaning "empress." However, Nero soon realized that he was not safe from his mother's lust for power and tried to kill her. He attempted three times to poison her. Then he sent her out into the Bay of Naples on a ship designed to sink, but she managed to swim ashore. Eventually Nero sent soldiers to her villa to kill her.

Agrippina poses for the sculptor with her son, the future emperor and absolute tyrant Nero.

Chronology

15 CE	Born in Rome.
39 CE	Exiled for plotting against her brother Caligula.
41 CE	Returns to Rome.
49 CE	Murders her husband and marries the Emperor Claudius.
54 CE	Claudius dies—probably murdered by Agrippina—and she takes power as regent.
59 CE	Murdered by her son Nero.

Nero

**Emperor
of Rome
37–68 CE**

*Known as the emperor who "fiddled while Rome burned,"
he was the last in the Julio-Claudian dynasty. He became a
dissolute and extremely cruel tyrant.*

With the possible exception of Caligula, Nero was the most unpleasant tyrant that the Roman Empire produced. Born Lucius Domitius Ahenobarbus, Nero's mother—Agrippina the Younger—changed his name to Nero Claudius Caesar when she married her uncle, the Roman emperor Claudius. When Claudius died in 54 CE—probably poisoned by Agrippina—the seventeen-year-old Nero was proclaimed emperor by the Senate and Praetorian Guard. Agrippina, however, effectively wielded power as regent.

By 59 CE, Nero had grown tired of his mother and, after several failed attempts, murdered her. In 62 CE, the prefect of the Praetorian Guard, Sextus Afranius Burrus, died and the Stoic philosopher Lucius Annaeus Seneca retired. They had been Nero's closest advisers and a restraining influence.

Burrus was replaced with the infamous Gaius Ofonius Tigellinus, who had been exiled in 39 CE by Caligula for adultery with Agrippina, and Nero had already come under the influence of Poppaea Sabina, the wife of his friend, who had become his mistress in 58 CE. Poppaea encouraged Nero to murder his wife Octavia, the daughter of Claudius, and in 62 CE Nero married Poppaea.

At Tigellinus's instigation, a series of treason laws removed anyone considered to be a threat. Meanwhile, military setbacks spawned an economic recession, while Nero and his wife lived in extravagant style.

In 64 CE a fire left much of Rome in ruins. Although Nero himself commanded the fire fighting, his artistic inclinations were well known and it was that said he sang or played the lyre as he watched the city burn. There was also a rumor that he had started the fire himself to clear the way for an extravagant palace called the Golden House, built at a time when public reconstruction should have been a priority. The fire also became the excuse for the first persecution of the newly emergent Christians.

In 65 CE Nero appeared on stage and sang for audiences—the equivalent of a modern-day President of the United States appearing in a mud-wrestling contest—and the conservative Romans were shocked and outraged. When a plot to assassinate Nero and replace him with Gaius Calpurnius Piso was uncovered, among the conspirators forced to commit suicide were Nero's old mentor Seneca and the poet Lucan.

In 67 CE, with Rome in crisis, Nero left the capital for an extravagant tour of

Chronology

37 CE	Born December 15 at Antrium, modern-day Anzio, Italy.
54 CE	Proclaimed emperor, but the real power stayed with his mother as regent.
59 CE	Murders his mother.
62 CE	Begins treason trials to purge enemies.
64 CE	Rome burns down while, some say, Nero fiddled; builds lavish palace and begins persecution of the Christians.
65 CE	Sings on the public stage; uncovers Pisonian conspiracy.
67 CE	Begins extravagant tour of Greece, leaving a freedman in charge in Rome; forces Corbulo to commit suicide.

Greece. Increasingly paranoid, he ordered the popular and successful general Gnaeus Domitius Corbulo to commit suicide. Fearing for their own lives, the governors of the Roman provinces went into open revolt. Their leader, Gaius Julius Vindex, said contempuously of Nero: "I have seen him on stage playing pregnant women and slaves about to be executed."

As the Senate forces close in on him, Nero opts for suicide rather than trial and certain execution.

Nero's reponse to their rebellion was reportedly: "I have only to appear and sing to have peace once more in Gaul."

The legions proclaimed Servius Supoicius Galba, the governor of Spain, emperor. The Senate then condemned Nero to die a slave's death, being whipped and crucified. When his Praetorian Guard turned against him, Nero fled. There are two versions of his death. In one, told by Roman historian Suetonius, he took his own life with a dagger on June 9, 68 CE. Tacitus, on the other hand, records that Nero reached the Greek islands in the guise of a red-haired prophet and leader of the poor. The governor of Cythnos had him arrested in 69 CE and carried out the sentence passed by the Senate. Whichever version is correct, it seems clear that Nero met a premature end as a direct result of his tyranny; he would not, however, be the last tyrant to hold power in Rome.

"I have seen him on stage playing pregnant women and slaves about to be executed."

15

Attila the Hun

The aggressive and ambitious chieftain of the nomadic Huns, Attila the Hun was known in his own time as "the scourge of God" for his savagery. He said of himself: "Where I have passed, the grass will not grow again."

Little is known of Attila the Hun's early life, but in 434 he and his brother Bleda inherited an empire that stretched from the Alps to the Baltic from their uncle Ruga, who already had a treaty with Rome. Attila and Bleda renewed the treaty, in the process upping the tribute Rome had to pay for peace to 700 pounds (318 kilograms) of gold a year.

The Huns turned their attention east, expanding their conquests into Scythia, Media, and Persia. But when in 439 the eastern emperor failed to pay his tribute Attila attacked, razing Singidunum—Belgrade—and other Balkan cities. A truce allowed the Romans to regroup, but in 443 Attila went on to destroy Naissus (Nis in Serbia) and Serdica (Sofia in Bulgaria). The attack on Naissus so devastated the place that, when Roman ambassadors passed through to meet with Attila eight years later, they said that the stench of death was still so great that no one could enter the city. They had to camp outside on the river, where they found the banks covered with human bones.

Attila turns from the invasion of Rome as heavenly figures appear in support of the besieged Pope Leo.

The Huns reached the walls of Constantinople and defeated the Romans in the east. Emperor Theodosius II was forced to pay the arrears of 6,000 pounds (2,722 kg) of gold, plus a tribute of 2,100 pounds (953 kg) a year from then on.

In 445 Attila assassinated his brother and made himself sole leader. He devastated the Balkans again in 447. As it would have been fruitless to try to besiege Constantinople with mounted archers, he drove southward into Greece, only to be stopped at Thermopylae. One chronicler said: "There was so much killing and bloodletting that no one could number the dead. The Huns pillaged the churches and monasteries, and slew the monks and virgins… They so devastated Thrace that it will never rise again."

A new treaty was concluded with the Eastern Empire in 449, ceding territory to the Huns. Then Attila turned his attention to the Western Empire. His excuse for breaking their treaty was that Honoria, the sister of the Emperor Valentinian, had sent him a ring. She had been having an affair with her steward, who had been executed. Pregnant, she begged the king of the Huns to rescue her. But he pretended that the ring was an offer of marriage and asked for half of the Western Empire as a dowry.

In the spring of 451, Attila forged an alliance with the Franks and Vandals and unleashed an attack on the heart of western Europe. In April he took Metz with an army of between 300,000 and 700,000. Rheims, Mainz, Strasbourg, Cologne, Worms, and Trier were destroyed. He was besieging Orleans when a Roman army under Flavius Aetius, supported by forces under the Visigothic king Theodoric I, arrived. In the bloody battle of Catalaunian, Theodoric was killed, but Flavius dealt Attila his one and only defeat.

Instead of retreating, he gathered his forces and invaded Italy the following year, sacking Aquilean, Milan, Padua, Verona, Brescia, and Bergamo. The survivors fled to a group of defensible islands in the Adriatic and founded Venice. It is said that Attila turned back before the gates of Rome because he was so impressed by the holiness of Pope Leo I, who came out of the city to parley. In fact, there was disease and famine in the area at the time and he may have feared the return of the Roman legions who had been fighting abroad.

With their booty, the Huns turned back toward the north. Along the way the forty-seven-year-old Attila took a new wife, named Ildico. After drinking heavily on his wedding day, he went to bed with his young bride. The next morning, he was found dead, drowned in the blood from a nosebleed.

Chronology	
*c.*406	Born.
434	Becomes joint king of the Huns with brother Bleda.
439	Attacks Eastern Roman Empire.
443	Destroys Belgrade, Nis, and Sofia; takes Philippolis; destroys Roman forces in the east.
445	Murders his brother.
447	Attacks Eastern Empire again.
449	Secures treaty with Constantinople.
451	Invades Gaul; defeated by Flavius Aetius in battle of the Catalaunian Plains.
452	Invades Italy; sacks northern cities.
453	Dies in his sleep on his wedding night.

"There was so much killing and bloodletting that no one could number the dead… They so devastated Thrace that it will never rise again."

Genghis Khan

Ruler of
the Mongols
1162?–1227

"I have committed many acts of cruelty and had an incalculable number of men killed, never knowing whether what I did was right. But I am indifferent to what people think of me." So said Genghis Khan in the thirteenth century.

The "tyrant's tyrant," Genghis began his murderous career at the age of twelve when he killed his brother in a dispute over a fish. By the age of thirty-three, he had risen to become the undisputed leader of the Mongol hordes—taking the name Genghis Khan, which means "universal ruler." In 1211, he began his conquest of imperial China, burning and pillaging every town and village on the way.

In 1212, Shah Muhammad staged a coup d'etat to become ruler of the neighboring Muslim empire of Khwarezm, covering Iran, Afghanistan, Turkmeniya, Uzbekistan, and Tadjikstan. Eager to maintain good relations with Khwarezm, Genghis sent a caravan to the shah carrying exquisite jade, ivory, gold bars, and felt made from perfect white camel hair. The three hundred caravaners were accompanied by a Mongolian noble who carried a message from the Khan. It read: "I know your power and the vast extent of your empire. I have the greatest desire to live in peace with you. I shall regard you as my son. For your part, you must know that I have conquered the Middle Kingdom and subdued all the tribes of the north. You know that my country is a swarm of warriors, a mine of silver, and that I have no need to covet further domains. We have equal interest in encouraging trade between our subjects."

The Shah was suspicious of this message. He accepted the Khan's gifts but sent his messenger back without a reply. Genghis sent a second caravan, this time consisting of five hundred camels, laden with beaver and sable furs. With it was Uquna, an official of the Mongolian court.

At the frontier town of Otrar, the local governor had a hundred of the caravanners—including Uquna—butchered and their cargo confiscated. Genghis had one more go at diplomacy. He sent a new emissary, this time a Muslim. The Shah had him put to death and his entourage returned with their heads shaven. As a final insult to the Khan, he confirmed the murderous governor of Otrar in office.

There could be only one response. In the summer of 1219, Genghis Khan assembled between 150,000 and 200,000 horsemen. Many were battle-hardened veterans of the conquest of China. Together with his horsemen, his best

Chronology

1162	Born.
1195	Becomes leader of the Mongols.
1211	Begins conquest of imperial China.
1217	Returns to Mongolia victorious with five hundred slaves.
1220	Massacres in Samarkand, Balkh, and Nessa.
1221	Four hundred slaves taken at Merv, the rest of the inhabitants put to death; populations of Neyshabur and Herat slaughtered.
1222	Massacres anyone who has returned to Balkh or Merv; population of Bamiyan slaughtered.
1223	Slaughters Russian knights at the battle of Kalka; loots Sudak, the kingdom of the Bulgars, and Kazakhstan.
1227	Dies on the shores of Lake Baikal, having been responsible for the death of around 20,000,000 people.

generals, his four sons, and one of his wives—Qulan, which means "she-ass"—Genghis Khan set off to make war.

Shah Muhammad's army easily outnumbered Genghis Khan's. But he did not know where the Mongols were going to attack so he deployed his men all along the border, a classic military blunder. Muhammad's men were so thinly spread that wherever the Mongols attacked they were bound to win. If the Shah had thought about it for a moment, he would have known where Genghis Khan was going to attack—at Otrar, of course, where the governor had killed his emissary.

Using siege engines captured from the Chinese, and also the Chinese expertise in gunpowder, the walled city of Otrar was soon captured and many of the unfortunate inhabitants killed, including the governor.

Genghis Khan, the "tyrant's tyrant."

The cities of Khwarezm continued to fall to Genghis's troops, and the Mongols soon reached the holy city of Bukhara, famed for its carpet weaving. When the Mongols attacked, the Turkish garrison tried to break out. They were hunted down and slaughtered. When the city was captured, the last of the defenders were put to death. The inhabitants were lined up and told to leave. Anyone remaining in the city was stabbed to death.

Genghis Khan himself rode into the great mosque, believing it to be the Shah's palace. Sacred Koranic books were thrown in the dirt. Hundreds of devout Muslims killed themselves rather than submit to the barbaric invaders. Among those who died by their own hand was the Imam of the Great Mosque.

The city was then burned to the ground. For dozens of years afterward Bukhara lay uninhabited. Thousands of corpses, too many to be buried, exuded diseases and those who lived in the surrounding region moved away. The irrigation ditches collapsed. The fields turned to desert and the animals, left to their own devices, perished. All that was left were the ruins.

Genghis Khan then turned on Samarkand. Behind him trudged a swelling army of prisoners, forced to work as slave laborers to destroy their own country. Samarkand was a city steeped in history. It had been ancient when Alexander the Great conquered it in 329 BCE. Now it was one of the foremost trading centers in the world.

Samarkand had recently been fortified. In the ramparts there were four great gates, symbolizing the city's dependence on trade. It had a huge garrison, manned largely by Turkish mercenaries.

Genghis Khan was impressed by the defenses too. When he arrived in the spring of 1220, he camped outside the city and waited for reinforcements. Meanwhile, he deployed a curtain of troops around the city. When two of his sons turned up with thousands of prisoners, they decided the best ploy was to impress the enemy with their numbers. They took the prisoners' clothes from them and dressed them as Mongols. Then, under close guard and with Mongol banners flying, they marched them toward the city walls.

The city's garrison charged the attackers. The Mongols turned and fled, leaving the unarmed prisoners to absorb the assault, then they turned and counter-attacked, hacking through the Turkish mercenaries. The survivors deserted, leaving the city defenseless.

The town's leaders came out to talk to the Mongols. Genghis Khan promised that all those who left the city would be spared. Some 50,000 citizens bought their freedom with a ransom that totaled 200,000 dinars. Those too poor to pay the ransom were taken as slave laborers by the Mongol units. Craftsmen were sent to Mongolia. Anyone who stayed behind was butchered. Once the city was empty, Samarkand was sacked. Part of the city was set on fire. Genghis Khan considered the Turkish mercenaries criminals and killed any he caught up with. One Persian chronicler says thirty thousand were massacred. It was said that when those who had paid the ransom returned to Samarkand there were so few of them they could only repopulate a quarter of the city.

The capital of Khwarezm was not Samarkand but Urgench, 300 miles (483 km) up the Amudar'ya River toward the Aral Sea. Again it was defended by Turkish mercenaries. But this time they were ready. They carefully stockpiled weapons, food, and water, ready for a long siege.

Genghis Khan promised that all those who left the city would be spared.

Genghis Khan charged his sons to take Urgench, naming one of them, Jochi, ruler of Khwarezm, so it was in his interests not to destroy the city completely. With them were three of the Khan's most experienced generals, and fifty thousand horsemen.

An emissary was sent demanding unconditional surrender. The offer was declined and the Mongols laid siege to the city. There were no boulders in the area for the catapults, so prisoners were sent out to find mulberry trees and their trunks were sawn up to make ammunition. Meanwhile, other prisoners, under fire from the city walls, began filling in the moat. It took twelve days. That done, sappers advanced under the cover of siege engines and started chipping away at the brickwork.

Soon after, the walls were breached. But, aware of what would happen to them if they were defeated, the defenders fought ferociously, house to house. Both sides used burning naphtha to set fire to houses where their foes took shelter, with a consequently high loss of life for the civilian inhabitants.

The Turkish mercenaries continued their stout defense from the ruins of the city, supported and supplied by the remaining inhabitants. After seven days, the Mongols lost their patience and torched the rest of the city. The Turks were forced to pull back but hundreds of civilians were burned to death. Eventually, members of the city council indicated that they wanted to parley. One begged the Mongols to have mercy on the brave men who had defended the city.

"We have seen the might of your wrath; now show us the measure of your pity," he said.

But the Mongols were in no mood for this kind of talk and the fighting continued.

"Everyone fought," wrote an Arab historian, "men, women, and children, and they went on fighting until the Mongols had taken the entire town, killed all the inhabitants, and pillaged everything there was to be found. Then they opened the dam and the waters of the river flooded the

A prisoner of the Mongols is flogged, watched by Genghis himself.

city and destroyed it completely… Those who escaped from the massacre were drowned or buried under the rubble. And then nothing remained but ruins and waves."

Genghis Khan was not at all happy about the destruction of Shah Muhammad's capital. The siege of Urgench had lasted six months, with much higher Mongolian losses than he was used to. His sons further incurred his wrath by seizing all the booty from what little remained of the city, leaving nothing for their father.

Meanwhile, the Khan's generals pursued Shah Muhammad, whose troops deserted in droves. City after city fell to the Mongols until the whole of Khwarezm was in their hands. Shah Muhammad died of pleurisy on the shores of the Caspian Sea, in what is now Azerbaijan.

Genghis Khan took a summer break at the oasis of Nasaf. Then he went north to Termez. When the city refused to surrender, he laid siege to it for seven days. When it fell, the usual massacre ensued.

Next he headed for the ancient city of Balkh, capital of the kingdom of Bactria in what is now northern Afghanistan. As a city, it had been known for three thousand years. Alexander the Great had occupied it and married his Princess Roxane there. But when the city surrendered to Genghis Khan on the understanding that its citizens would go unmolested, he went back on his promise and put thousands to the sword.

"Not a man, not an ear of corn; no scrap of food, not an item of clothing remained," it was said.

In February 1221, Genghis Khan's fourth son, Tolui, and seventy thousand horsemen arrived at Merv, now called Mary, in Turkmeniya. It was a rich city famed for its ceramics. Its fortifications were particularly impressive. Tolui and five hundred horsemen spent all day inspecting them. Twice he assaulted the city and was driven back. But the governor then surrendered, having received assurances that no one would come to harm.

Tolui did not keep his word. He evacuated the city and picked out four hundred craftsmen and some children to keep as slaves. The rest were put to the sword. One source says that Tolui left 700,000 corpses there. Another said he stopped counting after 1,300,000.

In Herat, after a siege that lasted eight days, only the mercenaries were massacred. But later, the populace revolted, killing the Mongol governor and the Khan's resident minister. In revenge, the Mongols slaughtered the population, then withdrew and waited. When survivors emerged from the rubble the Mongols went back and killed them too. One source says there were 1.3 million dead, another 2.4 million.

Mongol contingents were also sent back to Merv and Balkh to slaughter anyone who had returned to the cities they had laid waste. Next on the list was Bamiyan, the jewel of Khwarezm, a stop-off on the Silk Route and an unparalleled center of culture. The story goes that the city was betrayed by Princess Lala Qatun, whose father was trying to marry her off against her will. She sent word to Genghis telling him how the city's water supply could be turned off.

However, during the siege, Genghis's grandson was killed. Genghis was so angered by the loss of his grandson that he did not even stop to put his helmet on before he started slaughtering the enemy.

The entire population, predictably, was then massacred. Even Princess Lala Qatun was not spared: she was stoned to death for her treachery.

After the death of Shah Muhammad, power passed to his son, Prince Jalal ad-Din. With an army composed of Turkish mercenaries and Khwarezmian conscripts numbering around sixty thousand, he holed up in a fortress at Ghazi, 100 miles (160 km) south of Kabul. The Mongols attacked but, after losing a thousand men, were forced to withdraw.

The Khan's adopted brother was in charge of the assault. Short of men, he thought he would fool Prince Jalal into believing he had more men than he had. He mounted straw dummies on horseback and rode them up to his camp as if they were a relief army. The ruse did not work. The prince attacked. For the first time on Muslim territory, the Mongols suffered a defeat. When Genghis Khan heard of this, he leapt into the saddle. With fresh troops, he rode continuously for two days to reach Ghazi. By the time they reached Ghazi, a dispute had broken out between the Turkish mercenaries and the local troops and Prince Jalal was forced to withdraw. The city's inhabitants were deported or killed and its defenses destroyed.

The prince planned to escape to the Punjab but was caught with his back to the Indus River. There he surrounded himself with a square of troops and made a stand. But the Mongols steadily hacked away at his lines of defense. When he had only a handful of men left, the prince made a break for it and jumped off a cliff on horseback into the river. Genghis Khan was full of admiration—first for how the prince had saved his own life at the expense of those of his men, and then for the leap. He was an example to all Mongols, the Khan said, and was allowed to escape.

Genghis Khan was full of admiration for how the prince had spared his own life at the expense of those of his men.

Meanwhile, following the death of Shah Muhammad, the Khan's general Jebe had moved on northward into Georgia, defeating the Georgian cavalry, the mightiest in the region. Then he moved on into Russia.

At the battle of Kalka, the Mongols were attacked by eighty thousand knights under Prince Mstislav. The Mongols, numbering only twenty thousand, used a tried and tested tactic. After a short engagement, they withdrew, apparently in disorder. The Russians pursued them at high speed. This stretched out their army. Then, when they outnumbered the advance guard, the Mongols turned and fought. When the rest of the army arrived, they would come upon a scene of appalling butchery, which usually put them off fighting. If not, the Mongols slaughtered them as well.

The Russian knights wore steel armor and had shields, axes, swords, and lances, but were heavy and slow compared to the Mongol horsemen and they were easy prey for Mongolian archers. They were easily defeated and Prince Mstislav was captured. He was executed by being suffocated. As a mark of respect, the Mongols would not shed his blood. The rest of the Russian army were intimidated by Mstislav's defeat and withdrew. The Mongols went on to plunder the warehouses of Sudak in the Crimea. They looted the kingdom of the Bulgars, then they turned for home, cutting a swathe through Kazakhstan.

Genghis Khan himself returned to Mongolia and died in 1227. He left orders that, if anyone gazed on his coffin, the next coffin would be theirs.

Tamerlane

**Ruler of
Samarkand
1336–1405**

A Muslim of Turkic origins, Tamerlane took the motto of all true tyrants: "As there is but one God in heaven," he said, "there ought to be but one ruler on the earth."

Chronology

1336	Born at Kesh near Samarkand.
1366	Conquers Transoxania.
1370	Becomes ruler of Samarkand.
1380	Subdues Turkistan.
1383	Takes Herat, Persia.
1385	Completes conquest of Persia.
1387	Kills 70,000 inhabitants of Isfahan.
1391	Invades Russia.
1394	Conquers Iraq and Central Asia.
1395	Occupies Moscow.
1396	Subdues revolt in Persia.
1398	Invades India; destroys Delhi.
1401	Defeats Mamelukes; occupies Damascus; destroys Baghdad.
1404	Sets out to invade China.
1405	Dies February 19.

Born in Kesh, near Samarkand, in 1336, Timur was hit by an arrow while stealing sheep, leaving him partially paralyzed down his left-hand side. He became known as "Timur the Lame" or "Tamerlane" and rose to become chief minister of Transoxania—modern Uzbekistan—under the governor Ilyas Khoja in 1361. He soon rebelled and, with his brother-in-law Amir Husayn, defeated Khoja in 1364, completing the conquest of Transoxania by 1366.

In 1370, he turned against Husayn and killed him. Becoming ruler of Samarkand, he claimed sovereignty over the Mongols. Declaring himself a direct descendant of Genghis Khan, he set out to restore his lost empire with an army of 100,000 horsemen. Over the next ten years, he occupied Turkistan and sent troops into Russia to support Tokhtamysh, the Mongol Khan of the Crimea. They occupied Moscow and crushed the Lithuanians.

In 1383, Tamerlane turned his attention to Persia, completing his conquest in 1385. Over the next eight years, he conquered Iraq and Central Asia. In 1391, he defeated Tokhtamysh and his Golden Horde on the Russian steppes, defeating him again on the Kur River and occupying Moscow in 1395. He returned to Persia to put down an uprising, massacring entire cities and building pyramids of skulls.

In 1398 he crossed the Indus, defeating the Muslim rulers of Delhi at the battle of Panipat. He ordered the slaughter of 100,000 Indian soldiers then went on to massacre the inhabitants of Delhi. While he was in India, the Mameluke sultan of Egypt and the Ottoman sultan Bayezid I encroached on his territory. He set out to punish them and in 1401 he defeated the Mamelukes in Syria, slaughtering the inhabitants of Damascus.

Early in 1405, while on a campaign to conquer China, Tamerlane fell ill and died in Otrar, near Chimkent—modern Shymkent in Kazakhstan. His body was embalmed and returned to Samarkand.

Tamerlane is shown here in conclave with his military advisors.

Gian Galeazzo Visconti

Also known as Count of Valor or Conte di Virtù, the ambitious Gian Galeazzo Visconti brought his family dynasty to the peak of its powers, uniting all the Visconti lands.

**Duke of Milan
1351–1402**

Gian Galeazzo Visconti was the son of Galeazzo II Visconti, who ruled Milan jointly with his brother Bernabò. The Viscontis had been the rulers of Milan since 1262, when Ottone Visconti had become archbishop there. The family emblem was a snake—the symbol of cunning—devouring a man, an appropriate representation of the actions undertaken by family members.

Born in 1351, Gian Galeazzo improved his political standing in 1360 by marrying Isabella of Valois, daughter of the king of France. In 1378, his father died and Gian Galeazzo inherited the western half of the city, where he became a fearsome ruler. Bernabò was worse. When he rode through the streets, everyone had to kneel. Anyone who opposed him or even annoyed him was savagely punished. Bernabò had devised a program of torture that lasted forty days, which he published to put the fear of God into his subjects.

In 1382, Bernabò allied himself with the French prince Louis of Anjou, arranging for Louis' son to marry his daughter. Gian Galeazzo feared that this would increase Bernabò's power. Pretending to be on a pilgrimage, he invited Bernabò to meet him outside the city walls. There he had him seized and thrown into a dungeon, where he died a few months later, probably poisoned. Gian Galeazzo then united the two halves of Milan, with himself in complete control.

In 1387, Gian Galeazzo offered the hand of his own daughter to Louis, Duke of Orleans, the brother of the king of France. He threw the Scala dynasty out of Verona and seized the March of Treviso, north of Venice. In return for a bribe of 100,000 florins, the German King Wenceslas made him a hereditary prince of the Holy Roman Empire, appointing him Duke of Milan in 1395 and Count of Pavia in 1396.

He took over Pisa and Siena in 1399. Perugia and the other towns of Umbria fell to him in 1400, and he annexed Bologna in 1402. He now controlled the whole of northern Italy with the exception of Florence. Mustering his army for an attack on that city-state, he fell ill with the plague and died on September 3, 1402, having nearly realized his dream of uniting northern Italy into one kingdom.

Chronology	
1351	Born in Milan, Italy.
1360	Married to French king's daughter.
1378	Inherits the western half of Milan.
1382	Murders his uncle and takes control of eastern Milan.
1387	Seizes Verona and Treviso.
1395	Made Duke of Milan.
1399	Takes Pisa and Siena.
1400	Takes Perugia and the rest of Umbria.
1402	Takes Bologna; dies of plague on September 3 at Melegnano, near Milan.

Bernabò devised a program of torture that lasted forty days, which he published to put the fear of God into his subjects.

Tomas de Torquemada

**Grand Inquisitor
of Spain
1420–1498**

*It was Dominican friar Tomas de Torquemada who persuaded
King Ferdinand of Aragon and Queen Isabella of Castile to set
up the Spanish Inquisition, which tortured and killed in the name
of the Catholic Church.*

Born at Valladolid in Castile in 1420, Tomas de Torquemada was a nephew
of the celebrated theologian and cardinal Juan de Torquemada. In his early
youth he entered the Dominican monastery at Valladolid, and later was
appointed prior of the Monastery of Santa Cruz at Segovia, an office he held
for twenty-two years. The Infanta Isabella chose him as her confessor while
at Segovia. When she succeeded to the throne of Castile in 1474 he became
one of her most trusted and influential councillors. He prided himself on
living an extremely austere life: he did not eat meat and, unlike other
Dominicans, he refused to wear linen under his coarse habit, sometimes
wearing a hair shirt and always barefoot.

In 1483 he became Grand Inquisitor, first of Castile then of Aragon.
He wrote the twenty-eight articles that helped his inquisitors root out
sorcery, bigamy, and usury as well as heresy, blasphemy, and apostasy.
And he authorized the use of torture—up to and including the point of
death—to extract a confession. Although of Jewish extraction himself,
he persuaded Ferdinand and Isabella to expel all Jews from Spain and
spent much of his time persecuting Jews who had converted to Christianity.
In 1490, Torquemada staged a show trial of eight Jews accused of the
ritual murder of a Christian child, a common libel leveled at the Jews in
the Middle Ages. Although no evidence was offered against the accused,
and no body was found, they were found guilty
and burned at the stake. Torquemada used this to
argue that the Jews were a threat to Spain, and on
March 31, 1492 he persuaded Ferdinand and Isabella
to issue the Edict of Expulsion, which saw medieval
Europe's largest population of Jews made refugees
or killed.

*During Torquemada's
term of office as
Grand Inquisitor, over
two thousand heretics
were killed.*

Torture was Torquemada's great contribution to
the Inquisition. He gave orders that it should be used
in any case where heresy was "half proven"—that
is, an accusation had been laid but no confession
had been extracted. Simply being brought before the Inquisition was
enough. Being a "good Christian," Torquemada said that no blood must be
shed and his inquisitors usually avoided breaking the skin. However, he
conceded that people did die under torture. If this happened, the inquisitor
must immediately seek absolution from a fellow priest. Torquemada gave
all his priests the power to absolve one another of murder.

The word torture was not used. Prisoners were simply put to "The
Question." There were five carefully thought-out stages to The Question.
The first was the threat. The prisoner would already have heard about the

cruel methods that the Inquisition used, but the inquisitors outlined the tortures the victim faced, in the hope that fear alone would force a confession.

The second step was the journey to the torture chamber. The victim would be taken in a procession by candle light. The torture chamber would be dark and dismal, lit only by braziers, which would have their own terrifying significance. The victims would be given a little time to look around and see the devices that were employed.

In the third stage, the prisoner would be stripped, leaving them naked and vulnerable. The fourth stage was to introduce the victim to the particular instrument that was to be used on them. Only then, in the fifth and final stage,

Chronology

1420	Born in Valladolid, Spain.
1452	Becomes prior of the Monastery of Santa Cruz in Segovia.
1478	Persuades Ferdinand and Isabella to set up Spanish Inquisition.
1483	Becomes Grand Inquisitor.
1484	Issues 28 articles for the guidance of inquisitors.
1492	Expels Jews from Spain.
1494	Pope appoints assistant inquisitors to restraint him; retires due to ill health.
1498	Dies September 16 in Avila, Castile.

would the torture begin. Flogging, amputation, burning, the rack, water torture and other methods were all used.

It was technically against the law to repeat The Question. Once a victim had been tortured and survived, they could not be tortured again. However, the torture could continue day after day, week after week, with any interval merely being a "suspension."

Legally, confessions extracted under torture were not valid. So twenty-four hours later, the victim was taken back to the Holy Office, where their confession was read out. Under oath they had to swear that it was correct in every detail. If they did not, the torture, which had merely been suspended, would be resumed. If they did agree to the confession, the victim would be sent to the auto-da-fé (meaning "act of faith") and these public executions took place on Sundays or other holy days to allow more people the chance to watch.

During Torquemada's term of office as Grand Inquisitor, over two thousand heretics were killed in this way. His persecutions were so ruthless that Pope Alexander VI appointed four assistant inquisitors to restrain him. Although ill health forced him to retire in 1494, he continued to oversee the activities of the Inquisition from his monastery in Avila until 1498, when he died peacefully in his bed. He had lived to see the Muslims forced out of Granada as well as the expulsion of the Jews. At the time many people called him the "Savior of Spain."

Even after Torquemada's death, his Inquisition continued its grim work. It tortured and burned victims in Spain for the next two hundred years and it burned its last victim in the New World in 1836.

Vlad the Impaler

Count of Wallachia c.1431–1476

The inspiration for Bram Stoker's Dracula, *Vlad Tepes became ruler of Wallachia, directly to the south of Transylvania, in 1456. He did not drink blood but he did have at least 50,000 people—about one-tenth of the population of Wallachia—put to death.*

Descended from Basarab the Great, the fourteenth-century founder of the state of Wallachia, Vlad's father was honored by the Holy Roman Emperor Sigismund with membership of the Order of the Dragon—or Dracul in Wallachian. This meant his son was "son of a dragon," or Dracula.

Vlad was educated in the Wallachian court but, when Sigismund died, Vlad's father made a deal with the Turkish sultan to guarantee Wallachia's independence. Under this deal, the eleven-year-old Vlad and his six-year-old brother Radu were sent to Anatolia as hostages. They stayed there for six years.

In 1447 their father was assassinated and their elder brother was killed by a rival claimant to the throne who was backed by the Hungarians. The Turks did not want a Hungarian vassal in control of Wallachia, so they released Vlad who returned home, while Radu stayed on in Turkey. With the help of the Turks, Vlad seized the throne, but after two months he was forced to flee into exile in Moldavia. The new ruler of Wallachia then struck a deal with Turkey, so Vlad sought Hungarian backing and, eight years later, returned to Wallachia and seized the throne once more.

The following six years of his rule were characterized by needless cruelty. Five hundred Wallachian boyars who had opposed his rule were rounded up. The older ones were impaled; the younger ones worked to death building Vlad's mountain fortress at Poenari.

When in 1459 the merchants of Brasov refused to pay their taxes despite repeated warnings, Vlad led an assault on the town, burning an entire suburb and impaling numerous captives on Timpa Hill.

When Vlad fell out with the Hungarian king, he began torturing and killing Transylvanian merchants, impaling them and their families on wooden stakes. Although impalement had been practiced by the French, the Spanish, and the Turks, it would become synonymous with Vlad, who used impalement to punish even quite minor crimes in his drive for law and order. Vlad also used other terrible methods of execution, and would afterward display the corpses in public so everyone would learn a lesson. It is estimated that he killed anywhere between forty thousand and 100,000 people and it was said that over twenty thousand corpses were displayed outside his capital city, Târgoviste. His stern policy on law and

Portrait of Vlad Tepes from a painting in Castle Ambras in the Tyrol

order worked: to prove it, he had a gold cup placed on the drinking fountain in the main square of the capital. No one stole it.

It was the Turks, his principal enemy of the time, who named him "the impaling prince." Having fallen out with the Hungarians, Vlad had to turn once more to the Turks for support, but when Vlad refused to pay a tribute of 10,000 ducats and five hundred youths, the Ottoman sultan Mehmed II (the Conqueror) rode into Wallachia. Falling back in front of the invading army, Vlad burned villages, poisoned wells, and drove victims of infectious diseases into the Turkish camp. When the Turks finally reached Târgoviste, they were unprepared for the sight that greeted them.

"The Sultan's army came across a field with stakes, about 2 miles (3 kilometers) long and ½ mile (1 kilometer) wide," wrote the Greek historian Chalcondyles. "And there were large stakes on which they could see the impaled bodies… about twenty thousand of them… The Sultan, in wonder, kept saying that he could not conquer the country of a man who could do such terrible and unnatural things, and put his power and his subjects to such use. He also used to say that this man who did such things would be capable of worse."

Mehmed was so frightened he withdrew. Instead he sent Radu who, with defecting boyars and Turkish troops, drove Vlad back to his mountain fortress at Poenari. Vlad escaped across the Carpathians into Transylvania, but was arrested near Brasov by the Hungarian king Matthias Corvinus. Forged letters were circulated which indicated that it was Vlad who was a traitor to the Christian cause, not Radu.

Vlad ingratiated himself to his captors by converting from Orthodox Christianity to Catholicism. He was held under house arrest, though it is said that he kept his hand in by impaling rats and birds. When Radu died of syphilis in 1475, the throne of Wallachia fell into the hands of the rival Danesti clan. In 1476, with the backing of the Hungarians, Vlad returned to Wallachia again and reclaimed the throne. But that winter, the Turks invaded and Vlad was killed in battle. The circumstances of his death remain unclear. He might have been killed by his own side, who mistook him for a Turk, or he may have been assassinated by Basarab Laiota, who was to succeed him. Either way his severed head was taken by the Turks to Constantinople where it was stuck on a pole high above the city. It is thought that his body was taken by monks of the Snagov Monastery, whose renovation he had paid for some years earlier. They were said to have buried his body near the high altar, but an excavation in the 1930s failed to find it.

Stories of Vlad's cruelty circulated in German as early as 1463. Soon they spread throughout Europe, aided by the recent invention of the printing press. At least thirteen pamphlets detailing his crimes appeared between 1488 and 1521. Russian versions of the story praised Vlad's dedication to firm government, the Turks dwelled on his atrocities, whereas to the Wallachians he was a leader who repeatedly repelled the Turkish invaders.

Chronology

*c.*1431	Born Sighisoara in Transylvania.
1436	Moves to Târgoviste when his father Vlad Dracul becomes prince.
1442	Sent as hostage to the court of the Ottoman sultan.
1448	Returns to Wallachia; names himself prince, but is forced to flee.
1456-62	Institutes reign of terror on his return to Wallachia; flees to Hungary.
1476	Becomes ruler of Wallachia again, briefly, before being killed in December.

Francisco Pizarro

**Conqueror
of the Incas
c.1475–1541**

The illegitimate son of an army officer, Francisco Pizarro was abandoned by his parents. He had no schooling, could neither read nor write, and earned a living as a swineherd before he became a soldier. He went on to conquer the Incas.

In 1502, Francisco Pizarro sailed to Hispaniola to seek his fortune, then in 1510 joined an expedition to Colombia. On a second expedition with Nuñez de Balboa in 1513, he crossed the Isthmus of Panama and caught his first glimpse of the Pacific. When Balboa was beheaded by Pedrarias Dávila, Pizarro switched his allegiance to Dávila and was sent to trade with the natives down the Pacific coast. He helped Dávila subdue the warlike tribes in Panama and in 1520 undertook an expedition to Cacique Urraca, situated in the present Republic of Costa Rica.

In 1522, news of Hernán Cortés's slaughter of the Aztecs and the resulting haul of gold fired Pizarro with enthusiasm. With Diego de Almagro, another soldier of fortune, he set sail to begin a series of expeditions along the coast of South America. Conditions were appalling and many of his men died, but in 1528 he returned to Panama from Peru laden with gold. When the governor of Panama refused him permission to make further expeditions, Pizarro took his case to the king back in Spain. In return for delivering Peru to the crown, he was named a knight of Santiago and viceroy of whatever lands he might conquer.

In June 1530, Pizarro sailed for the empire of the Incas with four of his brothers, 180 men, and thirty-seven horses. After early difficulties, they succeeded in devastating a coastal settlement, despite the hospitality they had received from the locals. When reinforcements arrived, they invited the Inca ruler Atahuallpa to visit their camp. Pizarro then insisted that he accept Christianity and the sovereignty of the king of Spain. When Atahuallpa rejected both, throwing the Bible to the ground, Pizarro opened up with artillery on Atahuallpa's unarmed followers, massacring them.

The Inca army camped nearby was now leaderless and retreated into the interior. Atahuallpa himself was held for a ransom of enough gold and silver to fill the room he was being held in. When it was paid, Atahuallpa was forced to convert to Christianity and then strangled. Almagro then pushed on to take and devastate the Inca capital Cuzco, while Pizarro founded the Spanish capital Lima.

Pizarro had Manco Capac II crowned king of

Chronology

*c.*1475	Born at Trujillo, Extremadura, Castile, Spain.
1502	Sails for Hispaniola.
1510	Joins expedition to Colombia.
1513	Sees Pacific.
1522	Enters partnership with Almagro.
1528	Returns from Peru with gold; appointed viceroy of all the lands he conquers.
1530	Sails from Panama.
1532	Takes Atahuallpa, emperor of the Incas, hostage.
1533	Strangles Atahuallpa.
1535	Founds city of Lima.
1537	Almagro takes Inca capital of Cuzco.
1541	Pizarro assassinated June 26 in Lima.

the Incas in an attempt to control them. But Manco turned on his patron, and Lima was saved only by the arrival of some of Cortés's men.

Meanwhile Almagro had traveled on to Chile but, finding it poor, he returned to Peru where he rescued Pizarro's brothers from a siege in Cuzco, taking the town as his share of the spoils. Pizarro then sent troops from Lima, who defeated Almagro. He was imprisoned and executed. Pizarro spent the rest of his life trying to consolidate his power in Peru.

On June 26, 1541, Pizarro was assassinated by a group of Almagro supporters, led by Almagro's son.

Atahuallpa, under duress, agrees to convert to Christianity. Pizarro nevertheless had him strangled.

Hernán Cortés

The young Spanish nobleman Hernán Cortés destroyed the Aztec empire, turning against his Spanish masters to become ruler of New Spain, now known as Mexico.

Cortés conquered the Aztec empire with just five hundred men, sixteen horses, and a few cannon. Almost as important was his mistress, a slave called Malinche, later baptized as Doña Marina. She spoke both Mayan and the Aztec language Natuatl and acted crucially as his interpreter throughout the campaign.

The Aztecs had an inkling of their fate when, between 1507 and 1510, strange ships began to be seen off the coast of Mexico. Then came a series of ill omens. Although the Aztec ruler Motecuhzoma II simply executed anyone who reported portents of doom, it did no good. According to Aztec legends, the god Quetzalcoatl, the mythical ruler of the Toltecs, the Aztecs' precursors, had been exiled and would return in the year I Reed, according to the Aztec calendar. I Reed was 1519, the year Cortés arrived from Cuba.

Naturally Motecuhzoma assumed that they were gods and that their ships were wooden temples. He sent gold and magnificent costumes made out of feathers, in the hope that the gods would take the gifts and go. Instead Cortés seized the messengers and put them in chains. Cortés established himself at Veracruz and burned his ships so that his men could not flee, then began his march on the Aztec capital Tenochtitlán.

The Spanish had overwhelming military superiority. War for peoples of pre-Columbian Mexico was largely a ceremonial affair. They wore elaborate costumes and were armed only with a small sword made out of obsidian—volcanic glass. Their object was to capture as many of the enemy as possible to use as human sacrifices later. If a leader was killed or a temple captured, the loser capitulated immediately and talks began over the amount of tribute to be paid. However, Cortés slaughtered as many men as he could on the battlefield.

Motecuhzoma's only possible defense was guile. He tried to capture Cortés in an ambush at Cholula. But Cortés discovered the plan and massacred the citizens of Cholula. He destroyed the temple of Huitzilopochtli, the Aztec god of war, there and set up an image of the Virgin Mary instead.

Cortés established an alliance with the people of Tlaxcala, who had only recently been conquered by Motecuhzoma. They rebelled and more subject peoples rallied to Cortés. Hearing what had happened at Cholula, other Aztec cities surrendered without a fight and Cortés marched on Tenochtitlán unopposed.

Hernán Cortés, who led a tiny army that brutally conquered the mighty Aztec Empire in Mexico

Motecuhzoma had no choice but to greet the Spanish graciously. He lodged Cortés in the palace of Axayacatl, Motecuhzoma's father, which was packed with gold ornaments. The Spanish melted these down; the gold was shipped as bars and sent directly to Charles V in Spain, bypassing Cortés's commander, the governor of Cuba, Diego Velázquez. Cortés also demanded that Motecuhzoma swear allegiance to Charles V of Spain. He was to remain nominal ruler of the Aztecs while Cortés himself seized the reins of power, with the aim of becoming viceroy.

To reassert his authority, Velázquez sent a force of over a thousand under Panfilo de Narváez to bring Cortés to heel. Leaving a small force under Pedro de Alvardo in Tenochtitlán, Cortés headed back to the coast where he defeated Narváez and used his troops to swell his own ranks.

Meanwhile, in Tenochtitlán, the Aztecs were celebrating the festival of their war god Huitzilopochtli which, like all Aztec festivals, involved human sacrifice on an epic scale. Alvardo's men turned on the Aztecs and slaughtered as many as ten thousand priests and worshippers. When Cortés returned to Tenochtitlán, he found the city in a state of open warfare. He tried to calm the situation by getting Motecuhzoma to talk to his people, but the Aztecs stoned Motecuhzoma to death as a traitor.

Cortés grabbed as much gold and treasure as his men could carry and tried to make a run for it. The Aztecs ambushed them and Cortés escaped with just five hundred men; but he turned back and laid siege to the city.

The Aztecs put up fierce resistance. But for months, they were starved and harried. Finally they were defeated by an epidemic of smallpox brought by one of Narváez's soldiers. This killed Motecuhzoma's successor, his brother Cuitlahuac.

Cortés demolished Tenochtitlán, using the rubble to fill in the city's waterways that had served as streets. Mexico City was built on the ruins. The surviving Aztecs were used as slave labor in the gold and silver mines. They were decimated by two further epidemics of smallpox. Forcible conversion to Christianity destroyed what remained of their culture.

What little we know of the Aztecs comes from Cortés and his men, who were more interested in booty than scholarship, and the Franciscan friar Bernardino de Sahagún, who questioned the survivors in an attempt to learn something of the culture they had destroyed. His work was inhibited by the Inquisition, who investigated him for being too pro-native and confiscated his writings which, fortunately, resurfaced in the eighteenth century.

Cortés led an expedition to Honduras in 1524. Returning to Spain to plead his case in 1528, he was confirmed a captain general. In 1536, he led an expedition to Baja California, but when a viceroy was appointed he returned to Spain. Eventually he was given permission to return to New Spain, but died in Seville in 1547 before he could make the journey.

Chronology

1485	Born at Medellín, Castile, Spain.
1489	Attends University of Salamanca.
1504	Sails for the island of Hispaniola.
1509	Misses ill-fated expedition to mainland of South America.
1519	Lands in Mexico.
1520	After witnessing bloodthirsty Aztec rituals, his men slaughter 10,000.
1521	Besieges then razes the Aztec capital Tenochtitlán.
1524	Leads expedition to Honduras.
1528	Returns to Spain and is confirmed as captain general.
1530	Puts down civil unrest in New Spain.
1536	Leads expedition to Baja California.
1540	Returns to Spain once more.
1547	Dies December 2 in Seville.

Hernán Cortés

Henry VIII

King of
England
1491–1547

When Henry VIII came to the throne, he seemed to be the ideal king—young, fit, well educated, and handsome. Yet he was to become a bloody tyrant, famed for beheading two of his wives.

Although Henry was fond of hunting and playing tennis, he also wrote music and books—including an attack on Martin Luther, which earned him the title "Defender of the Faith" conferred on him by the pope. In 1502, his older brother Arthur died and he became heir to the throne. In 1509, Henry succeeded his father Henry VII, who had given England twenty-four years of peace after putting an end to the Wars of the Roses. Henry VIII saw that his first duty as king was to produce an heir to spare England from any further wars of succession.

It was also vital to England's interests that she maintain an alliance with Spain, so Henry married Arthur's widow, Catherine of Aragon, on the understanding that her former marriage had not been consummated. Although it was a marriage of political convenience, it also seems to have been a love match—at first, at least.

His father had left the royal household's finances in good order, so Henry VIII had no reason to call a parliament to raise taxes. He left the running of the government to his Lord Chancellor Thomas Wolsey, who exercised his powers through the court of Chancery and the court of the Star Chamber. In 1515, Wolsey was made a cardinal and papal legate to England, and he built Hampton Court Palace—which was far grander than anything the king possessed.

Henry concentrated his energies on foreign policy. A Scottish invasion was repelled at the Battle of Flodden in 1513 and he pursued several campaigns against France, concluding a peace at the Field of the Cloth of Gold in 1520. He also built up the Royal Navy, recalling Parliament in 1523 to pay for it. The following year, he imposed a special levy, which met with such fierce opposition that he was forced to rescind it, leaving both Henry and Wolsey both deeply unpopular and Henry practically bankrupt.

While Catherine had given birth to a live baby girl, Princess Mary, in 1516, she failed to give Henry the male heir he craved. Catherine was now in her forties and Henry had fallen in love with Anne Boleyn, the sister of a mistress who had borne him an illegitimate son. He appealed to the pope to grant him a divorce from Catherine on the grounds that a man was not allowed to marry his brother's widow, even though the pope had given Henry a special dispensation to do so.

Chronology

1491	Born June 28 in Greenwich, England.
1509	Succeeds to the throne April 22.
1527	Sends Cardinal Wolsey to seek divorce from Rome on his behalf.
1529	Ousts Wolsey after no divorce is forthcoming.
1533	Marries Anne Boleyn; breaks with Rome and becomes head of the Church of England.
1536	Executes Anne.
1536-40	Dissolves monasteries.
1542	Executes Catherine Howard.
1547	Dies January 28 in London.

Normally there would have been no problem, but at that time Pope Clement VII was under the control of the Holy Roman Emperor Charles V, Catherine's nephew. Unable to get a divorce, Henry went ahead and married Anne Boleyn without the pope's permission and broke with the Church of Rome, declaring himself to be supreme head of the Church in England. He closed down the English monasteries and seized their wealth, and killed all those who opposed him—including his own Lord Chancellor Sir Thomas More, who was executed for treason for refusing to acknowledge Henry as head of the Church of England. His chief minister Cardinal Wolsey fell into disfavor for failing to secure the divorce. He died before he could be executed and Henry took over his palace at Hampton Court.

Wolsey was replaced by Thomas Cromwell, who introduced legislation turning England toward Protestantism. Increasing government control caused a rebellion called the Pilgrimage of Grace in 1536. A thirty-thousand-strong rebel army was raised in the north. However, vague promises and assurances persuaded them to disband. Sporadic riots the following year allowed Henry's administration to pick off the opposition piecemeal. In all, some 220 to 250 rebels were executed.

When Anne also failed to produce a male heir, he accused her of adultery. She was sentenced to be burned alive, but Henry mercifully commuted the sentence to beheading and brought in a skilled swordsman from Calais to do the job. He was not so merciful to the five young men who were accused of being her lovers: after being tortured into confessing, they were hanged, drawn, and quartered.

Henry married Jane Seymour, who gave him a son, but he was a weakly child and Jane died shortly after. Henry then married a foreign princess, Anne of Cleves, in a match engineered by Thomas Cromwell in order to secure a Lutheran alliance in northern Europe, but found she was not to his taste, describing her dismissively as the "Flanders mare." Cromwell was arrested and executed, and Henry was able to enact legislation giving more power to the throne.

Henry's fifth wife, the nineteen-year-old Catherine Howard, was executed for adultery when it was discovered that she was not a virgin when she had married him. Francis Dereham, who had been her lover before her marriage, was hanged, drawn, and quartered, while Thomas Culpepper, who was found guilty of having an affair with Catherine after the marriage, only suffered the comparatively merciful punishment of beheading as he was one of Henry's favorites.

Henry married once again, for the sixth time, to Katherine Parr, who was to outlive him.

At once fascinating and threatening, Henry VIII glowers out of this portrait by court painter Holbein the Younger.

Mary I

Mary Tudor was the first queen to rule England in her own right. Her brutal persecution of Protestants earned her the nickname "Bloody Mary."

Mary I and her husband Philip II of Spain, in a portrait painted shortly after their wedding in 1554

The daughter of Henry VIII and Catherine of Aragon, Mary found herself declared illegitimate when Henry dissolved his marriage in 1533. She was stripped of her title of princess and forced to renounce her Catholic faith, though she continued to practice it secretly.

On the death of her half-brother, Edward VI, a Protestant insurrection put Lady Jane Grey on the English throne and Mary fled to Norfolk. However, the general feeling in the country was that Mary was the rightful heir, and she returned to London to a triumphal welcome. Lady Jane Grey—the "Nine Days' Queen"—was deposed after just two weeks and, along with her husband Lord Guildford Dudley, she was charged with high treason and executed.

Soon after her coronation Mary began to revive the Catholic Church, which had been banned under Henry VIII. When it became clear that she was going to marry the Catholic Philip, king of Spain, there was a Protestant rising in Kent under Sir Thomas Wyatt, leading to a march on London by the Kentishmen. Mary gave a rousing speech, which stirred the people of the capital to defend her, and the rebellion was defeated and its leaders executed.

Mary then married Philip, restored the Catholic creed, and began persecuting heretics. Some three hundred Protestants were burned at the stake. Her marriage to Philip embroiled England in an unpopular war with France, which lost her Calais, England's last toehold in France.

Lonely, childless, and hated, Mary died on November 17, 1558, to be succeeded by her half-sister Elizabeth I, a Protestant.

Chronology

1516	Born February 18 in Greenwich, England.
1533	Declared illegitimate and stripped of her title.
1534	Forced to abandon Catholic faith.
1544	Allowed to return to court and re-admitted to the succession.
1553	Ascends to the throne.
1554	Puts down Wyatt rebellion, executing leaders; marries Philip II of Spain.
1555–58	Burns some 300 Protestants at the stake.
1558	Loses Calais; dies childless on November 17 in London.

Catherine de'Medici

Catherine de'Medici, born into the powerful Medici family that ruled Florence almost continuously from 1434 to 1737, was a formidable influence in sixteenth-century France.

Regent of France 1519–1589

In 1533, Catherine de'Medici married the Dauphin, who became Henry II in 1547. Although he maintained a very public mistress, Diane of Poitiers, Catherine bore him ten children in ten years of marriage.

Henry II died in 1558 when he was accidentally hit on the head with a lance by one of his Scots Guards. In 1560, Catherine's eldest son Francis II—who had married Mary Queen of Scots—also died. The new king was Catherine's ten-year-old son Charles and she became regent.

At the time, France was split by a series of religious wars between the Catholics, who were backed by Spain, and the Protestants, led by a group called the Huguenots. Catherine attempted to end the conflict in 1572 by ordering the massacre of over four thousand Huguenots in Paris, in what became known as the St Bartholomew's Day Massacre. But instead of ending the conflict, the massacre provoked a renewal of hostilities.

Catherine became regent again when Charles IX died in 1574 and, during the reign of Henry III, continued dabbling in politics, stoking up religious conflict.

Chronology

1519	Born April 13 in Florence, Italy.
1533	Marries Henry, Duke of Orléans.
1547	Becomes queen consort.
1558	Husband Henry II dies.
1559	Son Francis II dies; Catherine becomes regent.
1572	Orders the murder of the Huguenots in the St Bartholomew's Day Massacre.
1574	Becomes regent once more.
1589	Dies January 5 at Blois in France.

Catherine surveys the bloody aftermath of the St Bartholemew's Day Massacre of the French Huguenots.

Ivan the Terrible

Tsar of Russia
1530–1584

Coming to the Muscovite throne at the age of three when his father died, Ivan lived in fear of the "boyars" and witnessed the terrible acts of torture and cruelty they performed in his name.

When his uncle Yuri challenged his right to the throne, Ivan was arrested, thrown in a dungeon, and left to starve. Ivan's mother, who was otherwise indifferent to him, assumed power as regent and had another of Ivan's uncles killed. Ivan's mother died a short time later, probably poisoned. Ivan was just eight years old. A week later his mother's consort, Prince Ivan Obolensky, was arrested and beaten to death by his jailers, and Obolensky's sister Agrafena, Ivan's beloved nurse, was sent to a convent.

Without Agrafena, Ivan had no one to turn to for help or advice. The boyars alternately neglected and abused him and his brother Yuri, a deaf-mute, leaving them hungry and in rags. Ivan was a beggar in his own palace. When a rivalry between two boyar families, the Shuiskys and the Belskys, escalated into a bloody feud, armed men roamed the palace, seeking out their enemies and often bursting into Ivan's quarters, which they smashed up and looted. Verbal and physical abuse, beatings, and murders were commonplace. Ivan was an intelligent, sensitive boy and an insatiable reader. Unable to strike back, he took out his frustrations on torturing small animals.

In 1539, the Shuiskys led a raid on the palace, rounding up a number of Ivan's remaining confidants. The loyal Fyodor Mishurin was executed and left on public display in a Moscow square. But on December 29, 1543, the thirteen-year-old Ivan suddenly realiated. He ordered the arrest of the sadistic Prince Andrew Shuisky and had him killed.

Although boyar rule had ended, the people of Moscow found themselves little better off. By the time he took power, Ivan was a disturbed young man and a heavy drinker. He threw dogs and cats from the Kremlin walls, enjoying seeing them suffer as they hit the ground. He roamed the streets with a gang, drinking, mugging old people, and having his victims strangled, hanged, buried alive, or thrown to the bears.

An excellent horseman, Ivan was fond of hunting: besides the thrill of the kill, he also enjoyed beating and robbing farmers. However, Ivan was also very devout. He would prostrate himself before icons and bang his head against the floor until his forehead was callused. He even made a public confession of his sins in Moscow and, in his quieter moments, devoted himself to books, mainly religious and historical texts.

Chronology

1530	Born August 25 at Kolomenskoye near Moscow.
1533	Succeeds father as Grand Prince of Moscow.
1546	Threatens to abdicate; is persuaded to stay on as absolute monarch.
1547	Becomes Tsar of Russia.
1560	Begins reign of terror.
1571	Defeated by Crimean Tartars who then raided Moscow.
1570	Orders massacre of 60,000 in Novgorod.
1581	Kills his own son.
1584	Dies March 18 in Moscow.

At the age of seventeen, Ivan was crowned Tsar of Russia. Within a few months, a mysterious fire destroyed much of Moscow. Ivan blamed the Glinskys—a prominent boyar family to which his mother belonged—and turned the mob against them. He then set about building an empire. He centralized government, ruling with the help of a "selected council," and expanded his territory to the east of the Urals. He reduced corruption and the remaining influence of the boyar families, and reformed the Church and the army, creating an elite force, the Streltsy. In 1558 he started trading directly with England.

He married Anastasia—a Romanov noble—who had a stabilizing effect on him. When she died in 1560, after bearing him six children, he became mentally unstable again. He smashed up furniture and banged his head on the floor in front of the court. Angry and depressed, he became increasingly paranoid and was convinced that the boyars had poisoned Anastasia. Despite a lack of evidence, he had a number of boyars tortured and executed. He dissolved the selected council and took full control, unleashing a reign of terror. Thousands were tortured and killed—even his closest advisers were imprisoned or exiled—though Ivan donated money to the Church to pray for the souls of his victims.

However, when in 1564 he announced he was going to abdicate, people begged him to stay, regarding rule by a mad tsar preferable to another dose of boyar rule. Ivan agreed to remain tsar on condition that he be paid a huge fee and given absolute power.

To enforce his rule Ivan formed the "Oprichniki," a hand-picked bunch of thugs who had to swear a personal oath of allegiance to Ivan. Dressed in black and riding black horses, they carried a dog's severed head on a pole as their emblem. The mere sight of the Oprichniki instilled fear in the populace. They killed anyone who earned Ivan's disapproval, and would not hesitate to burst into a church during mass and murder the priest.

Ivan fortified his residence and ran it along the lines of a monastery—though Christian liturgy alternated with the sadistic torture of his enemies. The Oprichniki were formed into a pseudomonastic order with Ivan as their abbot. They performed sacrilegious masses, followed by violent drunken

Ivan's castle at Ivangorod, on the Narva River, the border between Estonia and Russia

orgies and executions. Afterward he would throw himself down before the altar and repent, then rise and read sermons on the Christian virtues to his followers.

In 1570, Ivan sacked and burned the city of Novgorod and tortured or massacred sixty thousand of its citizens. A German mercenary wrote: "Mounting a horse and brandishing a spear, he charged in and ran people through while his son watched the entertainment." Men and women were tied to sleighs, which were pushed into the freezing waters of the Volkhov River. There were so many corpses they dammed the river and made it flood its banks. Novgorod never recovered. Later the city of Pskov suffered a similar fate.

After two years of bad harvests, Russia was hit by an epidemic of plague. Then in 1571, Moscow was devastated by a fire. Meanwhile the Swedes, Turks, Lithuanians, and Crimean Tartars massed on Russia's borders. Narva was lost, but Ivan managed to repel the Tartar invasion after they had sacked Moscow. Then suddenly, in 1572, Ivan dismissed the Oprichniki, reverted to the title of Prince of Moscow, and installed a Tartar prince on the throne, only to have him exiled after a year.

He would throw himself down before the altar and repent, then rise and read sermons on the Christian virtues to his followers.

His married life was just as eccentric. In 1561 he married a Circassian beauty, but soon tired of her. Two years after her death in 1569 he married a merchant's daughter, who died just two weeks after the wedding. He suspected she had been poisoned and he had her brother impaled. In 1575, he got rid of his fourth wife by sending her to a convent. His fifth wife was soon replaced by a sixth. When she was discovered with a lover, he was impaled under her window, and wife number six joined wife number four in the convent. When Ivan discovered that his seventh wife was not a virgin, he had her drowned. His eighth wife appears to have outlived him.

Despite his turbulent love life, Ivan maintained a good relationship with his eldest son, the young man he had entertained in Novgorod. But on November 19, 1581, Ivan had a row with his son's pregnant wife over the suitability of the clothes she was wearing. He beat her up, causing her to miscarry. Father and son then argued and, in a sudden fit of rage, Ivan struck his son on the head with his metal-tipped staff. The prince lay in a coma for several days before succumbing to the head wound. Ivan was overcome by grief, and allegedly never slept again, roaming his palace at night in an agony of remorse.

To the end of his life, Ivan was habitually bad-tempered and was seen to foam at the mouth like a horse. In his last years, he had to be carried on a litter. His body swelled, his skin peeled and gave off a terrible odor. As death neared, he took monastic vows.

In 1584, just as he was preparing to play a game of chess, Ivan suddenly fainted and died. Hardly a family in Russia had escaped his murderous rule unscathed and many had been eliminated completely. Farmers had fled their land in terror and countless acres had been reclaimed by the forests. The country would take centuries to recover from the activities of this most tyrannical of rulers.

Toyotomi Hideyoshi

Toyotomi Hideyoshi was instrumental in creating the idea of the samurai as a "warrior elite," a class apart who alone were allowed to carry weapons and wear armor.

Ruler of Japan 1536–1598

Hideyoshi was the Supreme Daimyo of Japan from 1590 to 1598 and completed the unification of the country. A foot soldier in the army of Oda Nobunga, who began the unification of Japan, Hideyoshi rose quickly through the ranks of the samurai, taking command when Nobunga committed suicide in 1582. In warfare he was ruthless. Once he diverted a river through an enemy's castle, drowning everyone inside. He did not hesitate to take the heads of a thousand enemy soldiers, and nor did he have any qualms about risking the lives of his own men.

When he took over the lands of other daimyos, he ordered them to destroy their fortifications and took their wives and children to Kyoto as hostages. For the offense of holding a single mercenary, he demanded the forfeit of three heads.

He drafted thousands of peasants for his enormous building projects, treating his workers harshly. He also levied punitive taxes, saying: "Treat peasants like sesame seeds; the more you squeeze, the more you get."

On one occasion some scribbling was detected on the gates of his palace. He had twenty suspects crucified. The notion of crucifixion seems to have amused him: in 1597, he had twenty-six Catholic priests crucified, who had come as missionaries to Japan.

Invading Korea in 1592 and 1597, he urged his men to mutilate the bodies of his enemy. Any officer who failed to carry out his orders or questioned them was summarily executed.

It was during Hideyoshi's rule that the tea ceremony became popular among the warrior caste, and on this too, he had firm views: when the inoffensive master of the tea ceremony Sen no Rikyu offended against the strict code, he was first exiled, then ordered to commit suicide.

When Hideyoshi's only son died in 1591, he named his twenty-three-year-old nephew Hidetsugu as his heir. When six months later a new son was unexpectedly born, Hidetsugu was no longer needed and in 1595 he was also sent into exile, then ordered to commit suicide. His young wife, their three children, and his thirty concubines were paraded through the streets of Kyoto, then publicly executed. Their bodies were thrown into a pit over which a stone was erected, bearing the legend: "Tomb of Traitors."

Chronology

1536	Born in Nakamura, Owari province, Japan.
1568	Joins Oda Nobunga's campaign to subjugate central Japan.
1582	Succeeds to command when Nobunga commits suicide.
1590	Becomes Supreme Daimyo—military dictator—of a unified Japan.
1592	Attacks Korea.
1595	Orders death of his heir and executes his entire household.
1597	Invades Korea again.
1598	Dies September 18 at Fushimi.

Boris Godunov

Boris Fyodorovich Godunov ruled Russia as a regent from 1585 to 1598 and as tsar until 1605. His story is told in Pushkin's play and Mussorgsky's opera, both called Boris Gudonov.

Son of a family of Tartar nobles, Boris Godunov was chief adviser to Ivan the Terrible. He married into the Muscovite nobility and married his daughter to Ivan's son and heir Fyodor.

When Ivan the Terrible died in 1584, the dim-witted Tsarevitch Fyodor succeeded him, but Godunov ruled as regent. He used Ivan's secret police to spread terror, and tortured, imprisoned, executed, or exiled all who opposed him.

In 1590, Muscovy went to war with Sweden, taking territory along the Gulf of Finland. In 1591, Fyodor's younger brother Dmitry was stabbed to death in mysterious circumstances. Then in early 1598, Fyodor died and the Russian Othodox Church begged Godunov to become tsar. He said that he would only accept the throne if it was conferred on him by a national assembly. An assembly was convened in February 1598 and he was duly elected.

He consolidated his grip on power by banishing the Romanovs and restricting the power of the nobility. But then, in 1601, famine struck the country. More than 100,000 of his subjects starved to death, while many others fled Moscow to join the Cossacks on the steppes.

Meanwhile, an army of Cossacks and Poles gathered in Poland under an adventurer who pretended to be the dead Dmitry. In 1604, they invaded southern Russia. Godunov's army slowed their advance on Moscow but, before they were defeated, Boris Godunov died. He was succeeded by his son, who was swiftly ousted by the Russian nobility and murdered. Russia then plunged into a period of civil war known as the "Time of Troubles," which only ended when a Romanov took the throne in 1613.

Opposite: *Boris Godunov is approached in the monastery to which he had retired, and entreated to accept the position of tsar.*

Chronology	
1551	Born.
1571	Marries into Muscovite nobility.
1580	Marries daughter to the Tsarevitch Fyodor.
1584	On death of Ivan the Terrible, becomes joint regent.
1586	Becomes sole regent after death of Fyodor's uncle.
1590	Starts war with Sweden.
1591	Prince Dmitry dies in mysterious circumstances.
1598	Fyodor dies; Godunov takes the throne.
1601–1603	Famine kills 100,000 and causes widespread unrest.
1604	Cossacks and Poles invade Russia.
1605	Dies April 23 in Moscow.

Aurangzeb

Aurangzeb, son of Emperor Shah Jahan, wrested India's throne from his father in June 1658, defeating three of his brothers in the process. For most of his long reign he conducted vigorous military campaigns to extend the frontiers of his vast Mughal empire, which reached its greatest extent under his rule.

Mughal emperor of India 1618–1707

The Mughal emperor Aurangzeb ruled a vast tract of what is now India and Pakistan. A passionate Muslim, he was intolerant of all other religions. He removed the tax-free status that his great-grandfather Akbar had granted the Hindus, destroying their temples and crushing their vassal states, which had previously enjoyed a semi-independent status. In 1675, he alienated the Sikhs by executing the Sikh Guru Tegh Bahadur when he refused to become a Muslim, which started a feud that would last for centuries.

Aurangzeb came to power by imprisoning his father Shah Jahan and executing the Crown Prince Dara Shukoh and two of his other brothers. Remaining on the throne for the next forty-nine years, he expanded his kingdom into the far south of India through the Deccan plain. Within his empire he enforced strict religious laws, razing the shrines and temples of other faiths and destroying many works of art in case they were worshipped as idols. He also insisted that words from the Koran were removed from the face of coins, in case they were touched by the hands of unbelievers.

His religious intolerance caused internal dissent which ultimately weakened his realm. The sheer vastness of the empire strained its army, its bureaucracy and its economy, and when Aurangzeb died in 1707, the empire became an easy target for invasion, first by the Persians, then by the British.

"I came alone and I go as a stranger. I do not know who I am, nor what I have been doing."

Aurangzeb, 1707

Chronology

1618	Born October 24 in Dohad, Madhya Pradesh, India.
1658	Seizes the throne.
1664	Plunders port of Surat.
1670	Plunders Surat, again.
1675	Arrests and executes Tegh Bahadur for refusing to become a Muslim.
1679	Taxes non-Muslims.
1687	Conquers Deccan kingdoms of Bijapur and Golconda.
1689	Destroys kingdom of Maratha.
1707	Dies March 3.

Opposite: *Mughal Emperor of India Aurangzeb prepares to climb up on his elephant, c.1666.*

Peter the Great

Pyotr Alexeyevich Romanov—Peter the Great—expanded the Tsardom of Russia into a vast empire and made it a leading Eastern European state, but his rule was cruel and violent.

Peter the Great beheads a rebel Streltsy noble, as the others are forced to look on and drink to their comrade's extinction.

Peter was just four years old when his father, Tsar Alexis, died. The son of a second marriage, he was strong and healthy, unlike his half-brother Fyodor III, who succeeded.

When Fyodor died childless in 1682, infighting broke out between the families of Alexis's two wives. Peter was named tsar, but the Moscow musketeers—the Streltsy—rebelled, forcing him to rule jointly with his feeble-minded half-brother Ivan V under the regency of Ivan's twenty-five-year-old sister Sophia. But in August 1689 Peter and his guardian, Prince Boris Golitsyn, succeeded in overthrowing Sophia and banishing her.

Between 1694 and 1697 Peter set about improving Russia's maritime position. He fought the Crimean Tartars and took control of Azov from the Turks, giving Russia access to crucial trading ports on the Black Sea.

He then undertook a European tour to secure allies against the Ottoman empire, visiting Germany, Holland, and Britain, but had to return when

the Streltsy staged another rebellion. Crushing it, he executed thousands of Streltsy, beheading many of them himself. He also got Sophia out of the way by forcing her into a convent, along with his wife, the beautiful Eudoxia, of whom he had tired.

Determined to modernize Russia, he replaced the Julian calendar with the Gregorian one, which had now been adopted across most of Europe. Because Europeans were clean-shaven, Peter introduced a beard tax in an effort to force the boyars—the traditional Russian nobility—to follow suit. This proved to be a very unpopular move.

Next Peter sought an outlet to the Baltic. He conscripted thirty-two thousand men and attacked the Swedes at Livonia in August 1700. However, he was soundly defeated at the battle of Narva that November by the Swedish king, Charles XII, losing over fifteen thousand men to the Swedes' 650. But he did not give up. Employing expert advisers, he defeated the Swedes at Erestfer and Hummelshof in 1702. Occupying the Neva valley, he built St Petersburg—his "window on the West"—on a frozen marsh on the Gulf of Finland.

In the summer of 1704, he besieged Narva, taking it on August 21. The Swedes reacted by invading Russia, pushing Peter all the way back to the central Ukraine. Once again the Russian winter got the better of the invaders and the Swedes were obliterated at the Battle of Poltava.

In 1711, he attacked the Turks in Moldavia. Then in 1714, he destroyed the Swedish fleet near Hangö, giving Russia a permanent hold on the Baltic.

Peter did transform Russia, building arms factories, military schools, canals, and shipyards using a workforce of over a million conscripts. When the people rebelled against a threefold increase in taxes to fund his adventures, he cracked down with executions, floggings, mutilation, and permanent exile to Siberia. The clergy were tortured to reveal the secrets of the confessional and murdered if they refused. Even Peter's own son Alexei rebelled against him. When the conspiracy was uncovered Alexei fled abroad, but was forcibly returned, imprisoned, and tortured to death.

In 1721, Peter was named Emperor of all the Russias. He seized control of the Church as patriarch, and spent the next two years fighting the Persians and pushing back Russia's Asian frontier. He died on February 8, 1725, having changed the face of Russia.

He executed thousands of Streltsy, beheading many of them himself.

Chronology

1672	Born May 30 in Moscow.
1676	Father Tsar Alexis dies, causing rivalry between the families of his two wives.
1682	Peter named tsar, but forced to rule jointly with Ivan V under regency of Sophia.
1689	Ousts Sophia.
1694–95	Leads military expedition to White Sea.
1695–96	Fights Crimean Tartars; takes Azov.
1697	Tours Europe.
1698	Returns to put down rebellion; sends Sophia to a nunnery.
1699	Drafts army of 32,000.
1700	Attacks Swedes; defeated at battle of Narva.
1702	Defeats Swedes at Erestfer and Hummelshof.
1703	Founds St Petersburg on May 16.
1704	Takes Narva.
1707	Sweden invades.
1709	Obliterates Swedes at battle of Poltava.
1711	Attacks Turks in Moldavia.
1714	Destroys Swedish fleet and takes control of Baltic.
1721	Baltic states ceded to Russia; named Emperor of all the Russias.
1722–23	Fights Persians.
1725	Dies February 8.

Catherine the Great

**Tsarina of
Russia
1729–1796**

Catherine the Great ruled Russia from 1762 to 1796. Like all the tsars, she was an absolute ruler and built on the reforms of Peter the Great to establish Russia as a great power.

Catherine was born on May 2, 1729, in the Prussian city of Stettin, now Szcezecin in Poland. At the age of sixteen she was married to her seventeen-year-old cousin Peter, the German-born grandson of Peter the Great and heir to the throne of Russia. However, Peter was an alcoholic, impotent, and feeble-minded.

When the Empress Elizabeth, Peter's aunt and Russia's reigning monarch, wanted Catherine to have children to continue the Romanov line, she arranged for Catherine to spend time with Sergei Saltykov, a Russian nobleman and accomplished womanizer. After two miscarriages, she gave birth to Paul, who was whisked away by Elizabeth and presented to the Russian people as heir to the throne.

Catherine then became romantically involved with a young Polish nobleman, Count Poniatowski, and they began an affair. It is likely that her daughter Anna Petrovna was fathered by the Polish count. When Peter found out about the affair he was furious and had Poniatowski sent back to Poland. Catherine however, had discovered a taste for illicit liaisons and replaced Poniatowski with a Russian officer in the Horse Guards, Count Grigori Orlov, with whom she would eventually have two children.

Peter was incensed by Catherine's infidelities and, when he came to the throne in 1761, he was determined to divorce her. But Peter was deeply unpopular. He made no effort to conceal his hatred of Russia and his love of all things German, and worse still, he worshipped Frederick II of Prussia, with whom Russia was currently at war. After just six months on the throne, Peter concluded a peace treaty with Frederick and started planning a disastrous war against Denmark.

Although Catherine had been born in Germany too, she was much more popular than her husband. Dressed in a lieutenant's uniform she rode to St Petersburg, where Count Orlov was stationed, with the army behind her, and proclaimed herself empress in Kazan Cathedral. Peter was arrested. He abdicated, but was murdered anyway eight days later by Orlov's brother Aleksei. Catherine then installed her old lover Stanislaw Poniatowski on the throne of Poland and went to war with Turkey.

Chronology

1729	Born May 2 in Stettin, Prussia.
1745	Marries heir to the Russian throne.
1761	Her husband becomes tsar.
1762	Proclaims herself empress; husband abdicates and is murdered; takes over lands and serfs belonging to the Church.
1764	Installs her lover Stanislaw Poniatowski on the Polish throne.
1767	Writes liberal constitution but fails to put it into practice.
1768	Goes to war with Turkey.
1774	Crushes Cossack rebellion.
1775	Tightens the grip of serfdom.
1783	Annexes Crimea.
1792	Annexes western Ukraine.
1795	Dismembers Poland.
1796	Dies November 6 at Tsarskoye Selo (now Pushkin) near St Petersburg.

The hardships imposed by the war caused discontent, added to by an outbreak of plague. The result was an uprising led by Yemelyan Pugachov, a Don Cossack who claimed to be the dead emperor Peter the Great. He was preparing to march on Moscow when the war with Turkey was won and Catherine was able to turn her full force against him. Pugachov was captured and beheaded, but the rebellion had left Catherine in fear of her people. Abandoning her liberal ideas, she tightened the grip of serfdom, largely under the influence of cavalry officer Prince Grigori Potemkin, who had distinguished himself in the war with Turkey and with whom she had an intense affair.

Potemkin organized the annexation of the Crimea from the Turks in 1783 and extended Russian territory along the shore of the Black Sea. Catherine then announced her intention of taking Constantinople.

However, in 1789 Catherine fell in love with twenty-two-year-old Platon Zubov and the ambitious Zubov became Potemkin's rival for power. After Potemkin died in 1791, Catherine went on to annex the western Ukraine and wipe Poland off the map, dividing it between Russia, Prussia, and Austria. In all, she added 200,000 square miles of territory to Russia. Catherine died at the age of sixty-seven, two days after suffering a massive stroke.

Catherine the Great was Russia's most famous and longest-reigning female ruler.

Louis XVI

Louis XVI was the last of a long line of tyrants. His grandfather Louis XIV was the very apotheosis of an absolute monarch, styling himself the "Sun King" and living in great splendor in Versailles while his people starved.

Louis XVI, king of France, meets his untimely end on the guillotine in the Place de la Revolution in Paris.

Economic conditions in France had not improved when Louis XVI came to the throne in 1774 at the age of twenty. Louis' chief financial officer, a man named Anne Robert Jacques Turgot, tried to reform the country's finances. He sought to replace the *corvée*—a feudal levy paid in labor—with a monetary tax, to ease the guild laws to encourage manufacturing and to cut the expenses of the monarchy. Turgot's reforms were rejected by the regional *parlements*, which consisted largely of the nobility who would have to pay the new tax. When the reforms failed, Turgot was dismissed.

The Seven Years' War and Louis' backing of the American rebels nearly bankrupted the country. Over one half of France's budget was dedicated to paying off the debt. Tax collection was catastrophically disorganized.

It varied from region to region and was undertaken by private businessmen who took a handsome profit. In the absence of a central exchequer, hundreds of government offices disbursed money, rendering it virtually impossible for anyone to have any idea of how much was coming in or going out. The accelerating financial crisis quickly caused inflation and, by 1789, over 80 percent of an average peasant's household income went on purchasing bread alone and unemployment in many parts of France had reached over 50 percent. And all the while Louis and his wife Marie-Antoinette continued to flaunt their extravagant lifestyle in front of the very people whose poverty they perpetuated.

Chronology

1754	Born August 23 in Versailles.
1770	Marries Austrian princess Marie-Antoinette.
1774	Ascends to throne May 10.
1789	Storming of the Bastille.
1791	Forced to become constitutional monarch; attempts to escape.
1792	Tuileries stormed; royal family imprisoned.
1793	Guillotined in the Place de la Revolution in Paris, January 21.

Louis tried to get his tax reform through the regional *parlements* again. They insisted that he call a national Estates-General for the first time since 1614. The assembly was made up of three Estates. The First Estate represented the nobility, the Second Estate the clergy, and the Third Estate the majority of people, whose economic power had increased considerably since the seventeenth century. As no adjustment had been made between the power of the estates, the Third Estate was easily outvoted, so its representatives walked out and formed the National Assembly, which demanded a new constitution.

As the situation in the country deteriorated with many regions now facing starvation, Louis was forced to publicly recognize the Assembly, while he mustered troops to dissolve it. Fearing that the Assembly was going to be suppressed, rioters took to the streets of Paris and on July 14, 1789, they stormed the Bastille—the fortress prison that was a symbol of Bourbon oppression—beginning the French Revolution. On that day, Louis wrote in his diary the single word: *Rien*—"Nothing happened."

Events quickly overtook him. On October 6, the king and his family were removed from Versailles and held under house arrest in the Tuileries palace in Paris. Louis was forced to accept a constitution limiting his powers. In June 1791 he tried to escape but was caught on the German border. He was returned to Paris, where he remained the constitutional king for another year. The outbreak of war with Austria in April 1792 made people suspicious of Marie-Antoinette, who was an Austrian princess, and probably responsible for Louis' worst excesses. While Louis began plotting to reverse the revolution, the National Assembly abolished the office of king, declaring France to be a republic. A mob stormed the Tuileries on August 10, 1792, taking the king and queen prisoner. They were put on trial for treason in front of the National Assembly and found guilty by a vote of 361 to 288, with seventy-two abstentions. Louis was guillotined in front of a cheering crowd in the Place de la Revolution—now the Place de la Concorde—on January 21, 1793. Marie-Antoinette followed him to the scaffold on October 16. Their son, named Louis XVII by French aristocrats in exile, died in prison.

On that day, Louis wrote in his diary the single word: Rien—"Nothing happened."

Maximilien Robespierre

Revolutionary
French leader
1758–1794

Leader of the Committee of Public Safety, Maximilien Robespierre was responsible for the bloody Reign of Terror that followed the French Revolution.

Born the son of a lawyer in Arras, he won a scholarship to study law in Paris. He was admired for his abilities, but his austerity and dedication won him few personal friends. Returning to his native Arras, he practiced law and gained a reputation for advocacy. A Jacobin, he came under the influence of Jean Jacques Rousseau's theories of democracy and deism, and Robespierre's emphasis on virtue—which in his mind meant civic morality—earned him the epithet "the Incorruptible." He even slept with a copy of Rousseau's *Social Contract* at his side.

Known for his neat dress and frugal ways, Robespierre was chosen to represent the city of Arras at the Estates-General conceded by Louis XVI in 1789 and oversaw the writing of the new constitution that was forced on the king. After Louis XVI fled in 1791, Robespierre called for the king's trial and subsequently for Louis' death. In 1792, Robespierre was elected to the Commune of Paris and represented the capital at the National Convention, the new governing body. Following the execution of the king, Robespierre called for further excesses. In 1793, he had a decree passed indicting twenty-nine leading moderates who had accused him of fostering a dictatorship. Robespierre was unrepentant. What was needed now, he said, was "a single will." That will was to be his.

Taking his place on the twelve-man Committee of Public Safety, he called for a revolutionary militia to combat counter-revolutionaries and grain hoarders. Massacres followed. The fledgling republic found itself embroiled in a civil war and under attack from outside by Britain, Austria, Spain, Portugal, Prussia, Russia, Sardinia, and Naples. On September 5, 1793—9 Thermidor, Year 1 in the Revolutionary calendar—the revolutionaries issued a decree making "terror" the order of the day. The enemies of the Revolution—nobles, churchmen, and those suspected of hoarding food and private property—were to be eliminated. There followed a wave of atrocities known as the Reign of Terror.

"A river of blood will now divide France from its enemies."

The first plan was to send the revolutionary army from Paris out into the countryside with a mobile guillotine. But Robespierre, who now headed the all-powerful Committee of Public Safety, wanted an army of half-a-million men to do the job and introduced conscription.

On September 17—21 Thermidor—the Committee passed the Law of Suspects, which allowed them to arrest and execute anyone suspected of antirevolutionary views.

"A river of blood will now divide France from its enemies," rejoiced Robespierre.

The Revolution was a product of the age of reason and, in Robespierre's eyes, organized religion was the enemy. The Committee sent agents out across the country to dechristianize the population. Churches and cemeteries were vandalized. The Bishop of Paris was forced to resign and Notre Dame cathedral was deconsecrated and renamed the Temple of Reason.

Lyon had rebelled against the Jacobins, but on October 9, after a bloody bombardment, the revolutionaries retook the city and renamed it Ville-Affranchie—Liberated Town. The houses of the rich were demolished and twenty to thirty rebels executed. Suspecting that the locals were being too lenient on their own, a revolutionary zealot named Mathieu Parein was sent to handle the situation. He ordered that those who had an income of thirty thousand livres or more had to hand it over immediately and that all vestiges of religion be obliterated. Houses were searched and mass executions began.

The guillotine became overworked. On 11 Nivôse, according to the scrupulous accounts the Jacobins kept, thirty-two heads were severed in twenty-five minutes. A week later, twelve heads were severed in just five minutes.

Mass shootings took place. As many as sixty prisoners were tied in a line with ropes and shot with cannon. Those who were not killed outright were finished off by the sword or rifle. The chief butcher, an actor named Dorfeuille, wrote to Paris boasting that he had killed 113 Lyonnais in a single day. Three days later he butchered 209 and he promised that another four or five hundred would "expiate their crimes with fire and shot." This was an underestimate. By the time the killing ended, 1,905 were dead—and the victims were not restricted to the rich, the aristocratic, and the clergy. The unemployed were also liquidated, along with anyone the Revolutionary Tribunal decided was a *fanatique*.

The ancient port of Marseilles in southeastern France, which had been rebaptized "Ville-Sans-Nom" (Town Without Name)—was similarly purged. After an insurrection in Vendée, a region on the Atlantic coastline in western France, the local agent wrote to the Committee of Public Safety in Paris describing their reprisals.

"There is no more Vendée, citizens," he said. "It has just perished under our free sword along with its women and children. I have just buried it in the marshes and mud of Savenay… I have no prisoners with which to reproach myself." The name Vendée was changed to Vengé—Avenged.

Two hundred prisoners were executed in Angers in December alone; two thousand at Saint-Florent, and at Pont-de-Cé and Avrillé, three to four thousand were shot in one long, relentless slaughter. At Nantes, a new method of execution, known as "vertical deportation," was developed. A flat-bottomed barge would be holed below the waterline, then a plank nailed over the hole to keep the boat temporarily afloat. Prisoners were put on the barge with their hands and feet tied. The barge would be taken out into the middle of the Loire where the executioner would pull out the plank and jump to safety on board a boat alongside. The barge would then go down taking the prisoners with it. Anyone attempting to escape drowning would be slashed with a saber.

The revolutionary army spread out across the country looking for

Chronology

1758	Born May 6 in Arras.
1789	Chosen to represent Arras at the National Assembly in Versailles.
1791	Oversees writing of constitution; calls for trial of Louis XVI.
1792	Calls for execution of Louis XVI.
1793	Instigates Reign of Terror.
1794	Executed July 28 in Paris.

Maximilien Robespierre

sedition. They would slaughter men, women, and children they suspected of harboring anti-Jacobin sympathies. Crops were also burned, farm animals slaughtered, barns and cottages demolished, and woods torched. Any town or village that had entertained anti-Jacobin troops would be razed. Terrorists planned to put arsenic in wells and enquiries were made about the possibilities of developing poison gas.

Twelve "infernal columns" were sent to "pacify" the countryside by killing everyone in their path. Entire families were slaughtered. One impeccable republican lost three of his sons as well as his son-in-law on the first visit of the Jacobins. They returned to massacre his remaining son, his wife, and their fifteen-year-old daughter. To save ammunition, General Cordeiller ordered his men to use the saber instead of guns.

At Gonnord, General Crouzat forced two hundred old people, along with mothers and their children, to kneel in front of a pit they had dug. They were shot so they fell into the grave.

In the Loire Valley, around a quarter of a million people were killed—that is a third of the entire population of the region. This figure does not include those who lost their lives taking part in the Revolution itself or during the subsequent battles fighting on the republican side.

Although Robespierre condemned the massacres in the provinces, he was master of his own bloodbath in Paris. By the time he made a speech on February 5, 1794, calling for the consolidation of democracy and the peaceful reign of constitutional laws, his Revolutionary Tribunal in Paris had already convicted and executed 238 men and thirty-one women, and a further 5,434 were in prison in Paris awaiting trial.

Entire families were guillotined, the older members forced to watch the younger being executed while awaiting their turn. When one prisoner stabbed himself to death in front of the Revolutionary Tribunal, the court ordered that his corpse be guillotined anyway. Revolutionary justice was not to be cheated.

The Revolution then began to consume its own. Anyone who opposed Robespierre was sentenced to "look through the republican window"—that is, put his head through the frame of the guillotine.

Robespierre executes his executioner after "all of France" has been put to death on the guillotine in this French cartoon.

When the great hero of the Revolution Georges Danton tried to call a halt to the Terror, he too was arrested and sent to be "shaved by the national razor." Meanwhile, Robespierre backtracked on the Revolution's avowed atheism. The dechristianizers, who Robespierre now viewed as immoral, paid for this sea-change on Robespierre's part with their lives. He then instituted the Festival of the Supreme Being, in which he took the leading role. This was not a return to belief in God, he explained—Nature was the "Supreme Being." But many people wondered whether Robespierre really thought that the "Supreme Being" was in fact Robespierre himself.

Robespierre saw himself as a missionary of virtue and believed he was using the guillotine as an instrument for the moral improvement of the nation. New crimes of "slandering patriotism," "seeking to inspire discouragement," "spreading false news," "depraving morals," "corrupting the public conscience," and "impairing the purity and energy of the revolutionary government" were introduced. To speed the course of justice, those accused were allowed no defense counsel and no witnesses could be called. The jury was made up of citizens who had to come to a fair and unbiased judgment without being distracted by such trifles. There were only two possible outcomes: acquittal or death, and it was the latter more often than not. Robespierre himself coined the slogan: "Clemency is parricide." The number of executions jumped from five a day in the new revolutionary month of Germinal to twenty-six in Messidor.

However, things had been going well for the French army and the danger from abroad had eased, and some republicans began to doubt the need for such draconian measures. Anyone against this new revolutionary justice must have something to hide, Robespierre argued, and promptly had them all investigated. Robespierre was so busy organizing the persecution that he did not realize that behind his back, some of the leading revolutionaries were mocking his cult of the Supreme Being.

On July 26, 1794—8 Thermidor, Year II—Robespierre made a speech calling for "more virtue" and his supporters called for his enemies to be sent *à la guillotine*. But the next day, critics pointed out that Robespierre had departed from protocol. Instead of speaking for the collective leadership, he had made a speech in his own name. Robespierre was lost for words at this accusation. In the silence a voice piped up: "See, the blood of Danton chokes him."

Quickly his opponents moved against him. They knew if they did not, they would soon face the guillotine themselves. Robespierre and his supporters were arrested on July 27—9 Thermidor. Under the circumstances, Robespierre could hardly ask for clemency. He tried to shoot himself, but only succeeded in shattering his jaw. Summarily tried, he went to the scaffold before a cheering mob in the Place de la Revolution the following morning.

Robespierre's death marked the end of the Reign of Terror. During this terrible time, in addition to those who were slaughtered in the countryside, at least 300,000 people were arrested; 17,000 were officially executed, and many more died in prison or without trial.

When one prisoner stabbed himself to death in front of the Revolutionary Tribunal, the court ordered that his corpse be guillotined anyway.

Dr José Gaspar Rodríguez Francia

Dictator of Paraguay 1766–1840

When Paraguay declared its independence from Spain and deposed the governor Don Bernardo de Velasco in 1811, the only native Paraguayan in the country qualified to sit on the junta which was hastily formed to run the country was Dr José Gaspar Rodríguez Francia.

Born in Asunción in 1766, Francia was the son of a Brazilian army officer who had come to Paraguay to grow tobacco. A francophile, he changed his name from the Portuguese França or Franza to Francia—the Spanish for France—and claimed French descent. After a couple of years at school under the Jesuits, he was sent to study theology at the University of Cordoba, in what is now Argentina.

Although Francia took no part in the split from Spain—and was probably against it—at Pedro Somellera's suggestion, he was picked to sit on the junta. As the other two junta members—army generals—knew nothing of government and the law, it was left to Francia to write a constitution. It ran to just four lines. When it was ratified by a hastily convened congress, Paraguay became the first independent republic in South America.

Concerned by the army's dominance over congress and disagreeing with his companions on the junta, Francia withdrew, leaving the government paralyzed. Once in the countryside he began to stir up discontent among the landowners, not a hard thing to do as Buenos Aires was at war with Spain and the Paraná River, essentially the only way for goods to get in and out of Paraguay, was closed. He also ingratiated himself with the local Guaraní Indians by treating those of Spanish blood with ostentatious contempt. Soon he was seen as the coming man.

Brother informed against brother; son against father; servant against master; husband against wife.

When the junta in Buenos Aires sent a diplomat to Asunción to invite Paraguay to join the confederation, Francia seized his moment. He put out the word that the Argentines were attempting by diplomacy what they had failed to do by force in an earlier invasion. Although in Francia's absence the junta had been expanded to five, they were still all Spaniards and the people did not trust them to put the interests of Paraguay first. They had no choice but to recall Francia. His price was to be allowed to rule alone. He first became consul, then Perpetual Dictator of Paraguay, known informally as "El Supremo." Francia's coup was not entirely unopposed. The troops under army captain Fulgencio Yegros rebelled and independence leader Pedro Juan Caballero intervened to restore order. Both were imprisoned. Caballero committed suicide in prison in 1821, while Yegros was executed the same year on Francia's orders.

Don Pedro Somellera, a fellow graduate of the University of Cordoba and Dr Francia's lifelong acquaintance, was arrested even though it was thanks to Somellera that Francia had been appointed to the junta. He was imprisoned along with his brother Benigno and the former Paraguayan governor Bernado de Velasco. Somellera was held incommunicado, but noticed that his cell door was often left open and he was fed information that a counter-revolution was being planned to restore de Velasco to the governorship. On the morning of September 29, 1814, soldiers took to the streets. But this was no counter-revolution; it was a trap. Those who rallied to their cause were shot down and hung from gallows, while the soldiers who had seemingly led the counter-revolution paraded under the gibbet, shouting patriotic slogans. With this simple ruse Francia got rid of any opposition. Somellera, knowing Francia well, had avoided falling into the trap and was allowed to leave the country. De Velasco died in prison.

Chronology	
1766	Born in Asunción, capital of Paraguay.
1811	Joins three-man junta to govern newly independent Republic of Paraguay.
1814	Seizes power as "El Supremo"—"Perpetual Dictator"—and seals off the country from the outside world. Begins reign of terror against anyone even suspected of harboring disloyal thoughts.
1840	El Supremo finally becomes El Difunto—"the deceased."

Francia immediately instituted a reign of terror, imprisoning on trumped-up charges anyone who criticized him. It was said that the blacksmiths in Asunción could not forge shackles fast enough. Anyone who had previously held political office in the country was arrested and their property seized, and the houses where Francia fancied that plots were being hatched were burnt down.

He set up a police force as well as a system of spying so effective that it was said he even knew the thoughts of the dying. Brother informed against brother; son against father; servant against master; husband against wife. Prisoners had no idea what they had been imprisoned for. No one dared ask. Some people were simply arrested and held until a ransom was paid, though they were rarely released even then. Few emerged from Francia's prisons. Prisoners were left there, ill-fed, unwashed, unkempt, with no medical attention until they died. Their relatives only knew they were still alive because they were permitted to send them food.

Francia also acted as chief executioner, issuing the bullets to his firing squads. These executions always took place first thing in the morning. The *banquillo*—the stool where the condemned man sat—was set up outside Francia's window. He watched to make sure the deed was done and insisted that the body remained outside his window all day to make sure the victim was dead before the family were allowed to take it away.

Like other dictators, Francia was terrified of assassination. Even though the cigars he smoked were made by his sister, every one was carefully unrolled to see if it contained poison—his sister was not above suspicion because he had imprisoned her husband, along with his own brother and another brother-in-law, and he had a nephew executed. He checked all the ingredients of his meals and made his own *yerba maté*—the local narcotic known as "Paraguayan Tea." No one was permitted to enter his presence with even so much as a cane in their hand or to approach Francia within six paces, and visitors had to keep their hands well away from their sides. Francia himself was never without a loaded pistol and unsheathed saber within easy reach. To guard again insurrection, no man in the army was promoted above the rank of captain. Nor did he trust his own government ministers, who were made to stand in the hot sun while he harangued them. The ministers were also imprisoned on a regular basis.

No one was allowed out on the street when Francia rode out with his escort. All shutters had to be closed along his route and orange trees, shrubs, and other places of concealment were destroyed. Anyone caught in the streets had to prostrate themselves or risked being cut down by saber. When Francia's horse shied at a barrel outside a house, the owner was arrested.

For several days, no one dared believe that Francia was really dead. People were afraid that it might be a trap.

After twenty-eight years in power, people began to believe that Francia was immortal. Then suddenly at the age of seventy-four he died. He caught a chill during a thunderstorm, which flooded his room, and took to his bed. When his doctor approached within the six-pace limit to examine him, Francia stabbed him with his saber, then had a fit. The doctor called for help, but the sergeant of the guard refused to enter the room without direct orders from Dr Francia. The doctor explained that Francia was unconscious and unable to speak, but the sergeant said: "Even so, if he comes round, he will punish me for disobedience." As a consequence, Francia died.

For several days, no one dared believe that Francia was really dead. People were afraid that it might be a trap. They feared they were being enticed into expressing relief or joy—only to bring down the wrath of the miraculously undead El Supremo. Indeed, Paraguayans feared even to mention his name decades after his death. He was known simply as "El Difunto"—the deceased.

Despite his contempt for religion, Dr Francia was laid out in state before the high altar of the cathedral in Asunción. A priest delivered a glowing eulogy which exhorted Paraguay to weep for the savior of the country and described Francia as the "guarantor of our national freedom." Meanwhile, Francia's rule was praised by misguided Scottish radical Thomas Carlyle for its "rigor."

The night after the eulogy, Dr Francia's body disappeared from the cathedral, giving rise to the legend that the devil had claimed its own. It was thought the old Spanish families of Paraguay had taken revenge by throwing his body into the river to be eaten by alligators.

Napoleon Bonaparte

**Emperor
of France
1769–1821**

*Both as first consul and self-made monarch, Napoleon would
brook no opposition either within France or outside it. He
reshaped his country and redrew the map of Europe, but his
plan for world domination was foiled by the British.*

Born Napoleone Buonparte in Ajaccio, Corsica, soon after France had
acquired the Mediterranean island from Genoa, at the age of ten he was
sent to military school in France where he found himself spurned as a
foreigner. After graduating, he was commissioned as an artillery officer. He
joined one of the revolutionary Jacobin Clubs in Grenoble and became
involved in Corsican nationalism. In 1792, he was elected lieutenant
colonel of the Ajaccio Volunteers, though after an unsuccessful action in
nearby Sardinia he fell out with the Corsican nationalists and had to flee to
Marseilles with his family.

When the French Revolution broke out, he joined the republicans
and helped drive the British out of their stronghold of Toulon. Having
distinguished himself as an artillery officer, he was appointed artillery
commander of the French Army of Italy. When Robespierre fell from
power, Napoleon was briefly imprisoned. Released, he took a post in
the Army of the Interior and in 1795 saved the new governing body, the
National Convention, with a "whiff of grapeshot," firing a cannon on the
crowds who opposed it.

As a reward, he was given command of the Army of Italy. He married
Joséphine de Beauharnais, a widow with two children, and changed
his name to the French spelling—Napoleon Bonaparte. He defeated

*"The Plum Pudding
in Danger"—
Napoleon (right)
and British Prime
Minister William Pitt
carve up the world
between them in this
famous cartoon by
James Gillray.*

the Austrian and Sardinian armies, and marched on Turin. As a result, Nice and Savoy were ceded to France. The following year, he kicked the Austrians out of Italy. He then set up a number of puppet governments in the Italian regions and looted the country's art treasures.

The Directory, which was then running France, asked him to invade England. Instead he proposed seizing Egypt as a stepping stone toward taking British India. On May 19, he sailed with 35,000 troops, landing at Alexandria. Agreeing to preserve Islamic law, he began restructuring the Egyptian government. But on August 1, 1798, the British, under Admiral Lord Nelson, destroyed his fleet in the Battle of the Nile, cutting him off from France, and in March the following year he was defeated in Syria by a Turkish army under British command.

By this time the French Army was afflicted with the plague and in August Napoleon abandoned his men and fled back to France. Arriving on October 14, he joined a coup d'état against the by now unpopular Directory on November 9, taking power as one of three consuls. Under the new constitution, he became first consul, with the power to hire and fire members of the council of state, government officials, and judges. He quickly consolidated his position to absolute ruler of France.

At that time, he was still a progressive. He improved education, encouraged industry, restructured the national debt, and codified the law into the Code Napoléon. However, he reintroduced Roman Catholicism as the state religion, began a building program using imperial Rome as its model, and muzzled the press. He kept control using his secret police and a network of spies.

He beat the Austrians again at the Battle of Marengo, signed a peace treaty with Britain and, on August 2, 1802, was made first consul for life. But this was not enough. He annexed Savoy-Piedmont and occupied the Helvetic Republic in Switzerland and the Batavian Republic in The Netherlands. And he sent an army to retake Haiti, which had seized its independence in a slave rebellion.

Napoleon returns to France from exile on the island of Elba, March 1815, to be greeted with adulation by the troops who are sent to arrest him.

Chronology

1769	Born August 15 in Ajaccio, Corsica.
1779–85	Attends military school in Brienne-le-Château and Paris.
1791	Joins a revolutionary Jacobin Club.
1792	Becomes lieutenant commander of Ajaccio Volunteers.
1793	Fights in Sardinia; family flees to Marseilles; drives British from Toulon, becoming national hero.
1794	Becomes artillery commander in French Army in Italy; imprisoned August 6 to September 14.
1795	Gives Parisian crowds a "whiff of grapeshot."
1796	Takes command of the Army of Italy; annexes Nice and Savoy; enters Milan.
1797	Defeats Austrians after long siege at Mantua; advances on Vienna sending Austrians to the peace table.
1798	Lands in Egypt; defeated by Nelson at the Battle of the Nile.
1799	Defeated in Syria; returns to France; stages coup d'état; appointed consul.
1800	Becomes first consul with dictatorial powers; defeats the Austrians at the Battle of Marengo.
1802	Created first consul for life.
1803	Prepares to invade England.
1804	Crowns himself emperor of France.
1805	Crowned king of Italy; defeats Austrians at Ulm; defeated by Nelson at the Battle of Trafalgar.
1806	Takes control of Germany.
1807	Defeats Russia; takes control of Poland.
1808	Installs his brother on the throne of Spain.
1809	Defeats Austria at the Battle of Wagram, taking Illyria and Galicia.
1812	Defeats Russians at the Battle of Borodino; enters Moscow to find it empty and on fire; forced to make disastrous retreat.
1813	Defeated at the Battle of the Nations.
1814	France invaded and Napoleon forced to abdicate; exiled on Elba.
1815	Escapes; returns to France; defeated at Waterloo; exiled on St Helena.
1821	Dies May 5.

Meanwhile, he sought to isolate France's traditional enemy—Britain—by restricting its trade. This brought war in May 1803 and Napoleon amassed an army of 170,000 ready to invade England. He used the discovery of an assassination plot to establish a hereditary dynasty. The Pope was summoned from Rome to crown him emperor of France, but when the moment came Napoleon seized the crown and crowned himself, and then crowned Joséphine empress. The following year he had himself crowned king of Italy, and installed members of his own and Joséphine's family on to various European thrones.

His plans to invade England thwarted by Britain's Royal Navy, Napoleon picked on the Austrians once more, defeating them outside Ulm between September 25 and October 20. However, on October 21 his fleet was beaten by his old nemesis the Royal Navy at the Battle of Trafalgar (off southwest Spain), ending any possibility of invading Britain. On November 13 he took Vienna and on December 2 he finished off the Austrians at the battle of Austerlitz. The peace treaty added Venice and Dalmatia to Napoleon's Italian kingdom.

He kept control using his secret police and a network of spies.

On July 12, 1806, he took the German states of the old Holy Roman Empire under his protection as the Confederation of the Rhine. To placate Britain, he offered to return Hanover to her control, provoking war with Prussia. But he defeated the Prussians decisively at Auerstadt and Jena on October 14 and took all the land between the Rhine and the Elbe.

War ensued with Russia, ending in a victory for Napoleon at Friedland, after which he took control of Poland. Now only the British stood between him and total domination of the European continent.

Unable to defeat the British at sea or invade, he tried a blockade. But the Portuguese—long-time allies of England—refused to comply. Napoleon marched on Portugal, but French troops in the Iberian Peninsula destabilized Spain. Napoleon forced King Charles IV and his son Ferdinand VII to abdicate on May 5 and 6, 1808, and Napoleon installed his brother Joseph Bonaparte on the Spanish throne. When Britain came to the aid of Portugal, embroiling Napoleon in the Peninsular War, Spain and Portugal's Latin American colonies seized the opportunity to declare their independence.

When the Empress Joséphine proved unable to give him a child, Napoleon divorced her and married Princess Marie-Louise, the daughter of the emperor of Austria, on April 2, 1810. She bore him a son, who was named King of Rome, but never reigned. Within months of the wedding France and Austria were at war again. Defeat at the Battle of Wagram on July 5–6 lost Austria the provinces of Illyria and Galicia.

However, in the Peninsular War, Napoleon found himself losing to the Duke of Wellington. His response was to tighten the trade embargo. When Russia refused to comply Napoleon invaded, beating the Russians at the Battle of Borodino on September 7, 1812. A week later he arrived in Moscow to find it deserted and on fire. As the Russian winter closed in, Napoleon had no alternative but to retreat, under the constant harassment of Russian troops who were better able to cope with the appalling conditions. Again Napoleon fled, leaving his army to its fate: most of his soldiers never returned from Russia.

Back in Paris, Napoleon mustered a new army, which beat the Russians and the Prussians at Lützen and Bautzen in May 1813, and defeated the Austrians again at Dresden in August. But he was defeated at the Battle of the Nations at Leipzig (October 16–19). Coalition forces invaded France the following year and on March 13, 1814, they took Paris. Napoleon abdicated on April 6 and was exiled to the island of Elba off Italy, then under British control.

He escaped, landing back in France, in Cannes, on March 1, 1815. The army rallied to him, but Napoleon now faced the combined forces of Britain, Prussia, Austria, and Russia. He decided to do battle with his nemesis the Duke of Wellington first. They met at Waterloo on June 18, 1815. Napoleon delayed the attack that morning to allow the field to dry out for his cavalry, a move that would prove fatal, allowing Prussian reinforcements under Gebhard von Blücher to arrive in the nick of time; and Napoleon was defeated.

This time he was exiled to Saint Helena, a remote British island in the South Atlantic, where he devoted himself to writing a self-serving memoir aimed at securing his legend. He died there on May 5, 1821, ostensibly of stomach cancer, though he may have been poisoned either purposely or accidentally as arsenic was a popular medicine at the time. He was buried on Saint Helena. Remains—probably not his—were returned to France in 1842 and housed in a magnificent tomb in Les Invalides in Paris.

Although Napoleon was honored, he had been so reckless with the lives of young Frenchmen that the country remained under-populated for decades to come.

Theodore II of Ethiopia

Theodore II ruled Ethiopia as emperor from 1855 to 1868. He was not of noble birth but a commoner who seized his native province, Kawara, then went on to gain the throne by fighting the feudal chiefs.

Emperor of Ethiopia c.1818–1868

Born Ras Kassa, he changed his name to Tewodros—or Theodore, in English—in 1855 when he united Ethiopia and became its emperor. At the time he was seen by many as Ethiopia's Peter the Great, as much for his hot temper and cruelty as his political ability.

Although cruel and ruthless, Theodore did introduce some reforms, including the banning of slavery, but he also sought to undermine the power of the Ethopian Church and the nobility, so that he would be the principal focus of the people's loyalty. To do this, he needed a modern army with modern weaponry, and to this end, Theodore forced foreigners living in Ethiopia to build him cannon. Eventually, he brought in armorers from Britain.

When a British engineer was killed, Theodore savagely slaughtered the culprits, but relations with Britain distinctly cooled. When a letter he had written to Queen Victoria went unanswered, he felt insulted and angry, and began to imprison British missionaries and officials. He also began torturing and slaughtering his own followers.

Finally, a British expeditionary force led by General Sir Robert Napier, and aided by dispossessed nobles, defeated Theodore's forces at Magdela on April 10, 1868. Theodore committed suicide three days later, using a pistol that Queen Victoria had sent him as a gift some years previously.

Theodore II, Ethiopia's "Peter the Great," pictured in worker pose.

Chronology

*c.*1818	Born Ras Kassa.
1855	Unites Ethopia and rules as Theodore II.
1855–67	Centralizes power, alienating Church and nobility; forces foreigners to produce arms.
1867	Takes Britons hostage.
1868	Defeated by General Sir Robert Napier at Magdela; commits suicide April 13.

Francisco Solano López

Francisco Solano López was the son of Carlos López, the successor to Dr Francia as Paraguayan dictator—and he would prove worse for the unfortunate Paraguayan nation than either of his predecessors.

López Jnr was a lifelong fan of Napoleon Bonaparte and admired the empire of Napoleon III. He would also read avidly *El Catecismo de San Alberto*, an account of the savage suppression of the insurrection of Tupac Amaru II, the last descendant of the Inca emperors, who, after being forced to witness the execution of his wife and sons, was himself mutilated and executed in an exceedingly cruel fashion.

Francisco was short, fat, ugly, barrel-chested, and bandy-legged. And like Carlos, he showed a predilection for extravagant uniforms, having them cut tight in a futile attempt to disguise his corpulence.

"His eyes, when pleased, had a mild expression; but when he was enraged the pupil seemed to dilate till it did not appear to be that of a human being, but rather a wild animal," wrote Ambassador Washburn undiplomatically. "He had, however, a gross animal look that was repulsive when in repose. His forehead was narrow and his head small, with the rear organs largely developed. His teeth were very much decayed, and so many of the front ones were gone as to render his articulation somewhat difficult and indistinct."

Chronology

1827	Born in Asunción on July 24.
1845	Named "Hero of Corrientes" for intervention in Argentine civil war.
1854	Visits Paris; meets Eliza Lynch; promises to make her "Empress of South America."
1855	Returns to Asunción with Eliza.
1862	Builds up army to 80,000 men.
1863	Succeeds to power.
1864	Seizes Brazilian steamer and invades the Matto Grosso.
1865	Overruns Corrientes and threatens Rio Grande do Sul; on May 1, Brazil, Argentina, and Uruguay sign "Triple Alliance" against Paraguay.
1866	Paraguayan army falls back to the fort of Humaitá after being defeated on land and on the river.
1868	Forced to retreat from Humaitá.
1870	Francisco killed at Cerro Corá.
1936	Francisco declared National Hero.
1961	Eliza Lynch declared National Heroine.

Washburn concluded that Francisco made no effort to clean his teeth and said those that remained were unwholesome in appearance and as black as the cigar he kept permanently clenched between them.

Francisco treated women with great cruelty and caused many a scandal. Eventually, even his father, Carlos, could no longer stomach him, and decided it might be wise for Francisco to leave the country for a while, until the various scandals had died down. He gave Francisco money and sent him to Europe to buy a navy, despite the fact that Paraguay is landlocked and had no need of one.

As Francisco and his entourage sprayed money around Paris like champagne, he came to the attention of an eighteen-year-old courtesan named Eliza Lynch, whom he promised to make the "Empress of South America." His Napoleonic dream was to unite South America under the rule of Paraguay, which was the richest country in the region at the time due to the sale of the narcotic *yerba maté*. Eliza encouraged Francisco's Napoleonic delusions. Born in County Cork, Ireland, Eliza was from a humble background—her family had emigrated to France to escape the Great Irish Famine—but she saw no reason why she should not become an empress.

Those who opposed him were imprisoned, tortured, and killed.

Francisco and Eliza went on a shopping trip around Europe, dining with the Pope and the notorious Queen Isabella II of Spain. When they arrived back in Paraguay, however, although Francisco was treated as a conquering hero, Eliza was snubbed as an "Irish prostitute." She was also dismayed by Asunción, which was little more than a shanty town—hardly an imperial capital. At her instigation, Francisco built a new customs house, a national library, an arsenal, a railway and station, a new cathedral, and an opera house—a replica of La Scala in Milan—although the roof was not completed until 1955, long after the dictator's death. Francisco also built himself a tomb—a replica of Napoleon Bonaparte's tomb in Paris.

He built up the army, which was soon six times the size of the pre-Civil War U.S. Army, and, as his father lay dying, staged a coup in which he arrested his brother and the two executors of Carlos's will. One of them died from maltreatment; the other—a Catholic priest—was tortured until he made a public statement, printed in the state newspaper, admitting every type of vice. When he emerged from jail, he was so changed he went on to become Francisco's chief torturer.

A congress was called to proclaim Francisco president. Those who opposed him were imprisoned, tortured, and killed. The congress also granted Francisco a massive pay rise and recognized Eliza as first lady. Francisco's next step was to invade Brazil, followed by an incursion into Argentinian territory.

Argentina and Brazil, although traditional enemies, recognized that Francisco was little better than a mad dog, and soon joined forces with Uruguay in a triple alliance against Paraguay.

Francisco was an international pariah for ignoring the diplomatic niceties and not making a formal declaration of war before attacking. Paraguay was blockaded and soon the Paraguayans were starving. Even so Francisco rejected all peace overtures. Any military setback was viewed as disloyalty and punished with torture and execution, though Francisco himself was terrified of bullets and cowered inside a fortified casement. He also became increasingly paranoid, seeing conspiracies everywhere. As a result he killed more of his own men than the Brazilians and Argentines, who prosecuted the war with extreme caution.

After three years of war, the Brazilian navy forced its way past the Paraguayan fort of Humaitá on the Paraguay River and Francisco was forced to withdraw. More hastily constructed earth forts were built further upriver, but each in turn was overtaken. Asunción was evacuated and the entire population of Paraguay was marched into the interior. Those who could not keep up were killed. Many died of hunger while Francisco, Eliza, and their children ate gourmet meals from the best china and drank champagne from crystal glasses. Periodically, the column would stop to allow trials to be conducted when Francisco suspected further

Francisco Solano Lopez in military uniform, complete with decorations to which he was not entitled.

conspiracies. Hundreds were slaughtered. Francisco had his two brothers tortured and executed. His two sisters were imprisoned in cages on the back of buffalo carts and his aging mother regularly flogged until she said that he was her only legitimate son. Francisco also took time off from his retreat to have himself canonized by compliant priests.

On March 1, 1870, the Brazilians, led by the Comte d'Eu, husband of Isabel, Princess Imperial of Brazil, caught up with the retreating column at Cerro Corá in the remote northeast corner of the country. Francisco fled and was caught fording a small stream. When he refused to surrender, he was shot and killed—possibly by a Paraguayan.

More than a million people died in the war, making it the costliest in the Americas in terms of loss of human life. Virtually the entire male population of Paraguay was wiped out.

During the war Francisco and, to a greater extent, Eliza looted the country. She sent the entire treasure abroad, robbing the womenfolk of their jewels, stealing land, pillaging houses, and stripping churches. Caught fleeing through the jungle in a ball gown, she was forced to dig the graves of Francisco and her oldest son, who had been cut down defending his mother, with her bare hands. But she was a charismatic woman, and the Brazilians took pity on her, smuggling her out of the country. She returned to London, where, despite her vast, stolen riches, she continued suing the Paraguayan and Argentine governments for other goods she claimed they were withholding. Eventually she returned to France, and died in Paris in 1881, where she was buried in Père Lachaise cemetery.

After another disastrous war, this time against Bolivia, in the 1930s, Colonel Rafael Franco seized power in Asunción, making Paraguay Latin America's first Fascist state. Remains—probably not Francisco's—were disinterred from Cerro Corá and brought to Asunción to be laid to rest with all due ceremony in the Panteón de los Héroes, as Francisco's replica of Napoleon's tomb is now named.

In a final postscript to the story, in 1961, the new dictator of Paraguay, General Alfredo Stroessner, decided to repatriate Eliza Lynch. The story goes that a Lebanese drug-dealer seeking to ingratiate himself with the Stroessner regime climbed over the wall of Père Lachaise cemetery one night and dug up the body, although it is likely that he too had exhumed the wrong remains. He smuggled them back to Paraguay in a coffin full of hash. Stroessner declared Eliza a National Heroine and planned to have her laid to rest alongside Francisco in the Panteón de los Héroes. But, at the last moment, the Catholic Church objected as the couple had not been married. They gathered dust for nine years in the Museo Lynch—which was little more than a broom cupboard on the first floor of the ministry of defense. Then on March 1, 1970, the hundredth anniversary of Paraguay's defeat in the War of the Triple Alliance, they were interred with due ceremony in the tallest marble mausoleum in South America in the national cemetery at La Recollecta. Huge statues of Francisco and Eliza now dominate Asunción. Paraguay, once the richest country in the region, has never recovered from their attentions.

More than a million people had died in the war, making it the bloodiest war in the Americas.

Leopold II

King of
Belgium
1835–1909

Belgium was only established as a nation in 1831, so it was a late starter in the race to build an empire. However, its second king, Leopold II, was an ambitious man...

Like the rest of Europe at that time, Leopold turned his eyes to Africa. He paid Henry Morton Stanley—who famously rescued the Scottish missionary Dr Livingstone—to explore the Congo. This led to the establishment of the Congo Free State, under the personal sovereignty of Leopold, in 1885. However, reports of the atrocities committed in Leopold's name there appalled the world and the Belgian state itself forced Leopold to hand over the Congo in 1908.

The Congo was rich in ivory, but even richer in "black ivory"—slaves. Although the British had outlawed slavery in 1833 and sent the Royal Navy into the Atlantic to stop the western trade, the trade to the east still flourished. Indeed, the slave trade was only outlawed in the Arabian Peninsula in 1970.

Although Leopold publicly issued antislavery edicts, he made Tippu Tip, a slave trader from Zanzibar, governor of the Congo's eastern province, at the same time "buying" the "freedom" of several thousand of Tippu Tip's slaves, who were then press-ganged into the Force Publique, the Congo's militia, and used to enslave the rest of the population.

There is an eyewitness account of what it was like to be taken into slavery by Leopold's men. It comes from a woman named Ilanga. She told an American journalist: "A large band of soldiers came to the village, and ran into the houses and dragged the people out. Three or four came to our house and caught hold of me, my husband Oleka, and my sister Katinga. We were all crying, for we knew that we were to be taken away as slaves. The soldiers beat us with the iron sticks from their guns and forced us to march to the camp of Kibalanga..."

"We then set off marching very quickly. My sister Katinga had her baby in her arms, and was not forced to carry a basket. But my husband Oleka was made to carry a goat. We marched until the afternoon, when we camped near a stream. We were glad to be able to have a drink there because we were very thirsty. But the soldiers gave us nothing to eat... The next day we continued the march, and when we camped at noon were given some maize and plantains, which had been taken from near a deserted village—the people had run away. It continued like this for five days. On the sixth day we became very weak from lack of food and from constant marching and from sleeping on damp grass. My husband, who marched behind with a goat, could not stand up any longer. So he sat down beside the path and refused to walk any more. The soldiers beat him, but still he refused to move. Then one of them struck him on the head with the butt of his rifle and he sprawled on the ground... and then I saw him no more. We had passed over the brow of a hill and he was out of sight. Many of the young men were killed in the same way... After ten days, we came

Leopold II

to the great water… and were taken in canoes across to the white men's town at Nyangwe."

Leopold ordered that children be separated from their parents and organized into three children's colonies where they would be taught Christianity and be trained as soldiers. But the missionaries and the colonies said that they should only take orphans. The Force Publique took this as an excuse to butcher the children's parents then force march the children to the colonies. Thousands perished. Of a column of 108 boys on

Leopold II, clutching his moneybags, cowers behind his soldiery in this cartoon by Condé for Vanity Fair (1869).

a forced march to a state colony at Boma in 1892, only sixty-two made it to their destination.

In the 1890s, there was a rubber boom—and the Congo was full of wild rubber, which came from vines, rather than trees. However, it would need vast manpower to harvest and brutal methods were adopted. According to the British vice consul: "The Force Publique would arrive in canoes at a village, the inhabitants of which invariably bolted on their arrival. The soldiers were then landed, and commenced looting, taking all the chickens, grain, etc., out of the houses. After this they attacked the natives until able to seize their women. These women were kept as hostages until the chief of the district brought the required number of kilograms of rubber. The rubber having been brought, the women were sold back to their owners for a couple of goats apiece, and so [they] continued from village to village."

The wife of any man refusing to collect rubber would be killed. This method of collecting rubber was recommended by the official manuals handed out in Africa. Once the system had been set up, every village was assigned a quota. This was usually three to four kilos of dried rubber per adult male per fortnight. Hundreds of thousands of men were conscripted this way. They were overseen by the Force Publique who built garrisons throughout the rubber-growing areas. Men had to carry their heavy load of rubber for miles to deliver it to the company agents. They would be paid in trinkets or a few spoonfuls of salt. One chief was paid in people.

Leopold wanted to open the country up with a railway. Of the 540 Chinese construction workers brought in from Hong Kong and Macao in 1892, three hundred died on the job or ran away into the forests. Several hundred workers came in from Barbados. When they realized they were in the Congo, they rioted. The soldiers opened fire on them. The survivors were taken to the railhead and put to work. Tropical diseases, lack of food, no shelter, relentless floggings, engines that ran off the track, and boxcars full of dynamite that exploded cost the lives of nearly two thouand men in the eight-year construction of the first stretch of track.

"As we progressed, a line of smoke hung over the jungle for many miles, announcing to the natives far and wide that civilization was dawning..."

News of what was happening in the Congo began to get out. In 1897, a Swedish Baptist missionary told a meeting in London that Force Publique soldiers were rewarded for the number of severed hands from their victims. A soldier had told him: "The Commissioner has promised us if we have plenty of hands he will shorten our service. I have brought in plenty of hands already, and I expect my time of service will soon be finished."

The British press were already gunning for Leopold. In 1895, a Belgian officer had "dared to kill an Englishman"—actually the victim was an Irishman who had "gone native" and married an African woman. When his ivory business challenged Leopold's monopoly, the Force Publique was sent. They hanged the Irishman, and the London press howled in outrage.

Leopold countered the bad press he was getting by creating the Commission for the Protection of the Natives, comprising six Belgian Catholics and six foreign missionaries. But he cleverly picked commissioners who lived so far apart that the commission only met twice and then only three attended.

The world's fair took place in Brussels in 1897. The Belgian exhibit included 267 Africans brought from the Congo, living happily in an African village set up for them in a park in Brussels. Ninety of them were members of the Force Publique. At a gala dinner, one of the Force's sergeants proposed a toast to King Leopold.

In the scramble to fulfil quotas the rubber vines were killed off. The Budja tribe rebelled, killing thirty soldiers, then fled. A punitive expedition was sent against them, led by an American rubber agent named Edgar Canisius.

"As our party moved through village after village, a party of men had been detailed with torches to fire every hut," he wrote. "As we progressed, a line of smoke hung over the jungle for many miles, announcing to the natives far and wide that civilization was dawning… The porters had an especially hard time, for many of them were chained together by the neck. They carried our boxes slung on poles, and when one fell down he usually brought down all his companions on the same chain. Many of the poor wretches became so exhausted by this kind of marching that they could be urged forward only by blows from rifles. Some had their shoulders so chafed by the poles that they literally shrieked with pain."

Chronology

1835	Born April 9 in Brussels.
1865	Succeeds his father, Leopold I, to the Belgian throne.
1876	Backs Sir Henry Morton Stanley's expedition to explore the Congo.
1885	Gains U.S. recognition of his personal sovereignty over the Congo Free State.
1892	Rebellion of railway workers put down by gunfire; 54 boys die on death march.
1895	British press in uproar when one Irish subject killed by Belgians.
1897	Swedish missionary tells meeting in London that soldiers were rewarded for collecting severed hands.
1899	British vice consul reports on brutality of the rubber trade in the Congo.
1901	Queen Victoria's funeral; Leopold grows increasingly unpopular.
1904	Investigation exposes the full horrors of the rubber trade in the Congo.
1908	Leopold forced to sell the Congo to the Belgian state.
1909	Dies December 17 in Belgium.

By the time Canisius caught up with the Budjas, the porters were done for and his prisoners had to take over. "All were compelled to carry heavy loads, each of which required two men to transport… until they finally succumbed to starvation and smallpox."

Roger Casement, the Irish nationalist later executed for treason, was then working for the Foreign Office. He was sent to the Congo as consul and reported back the brutalities he had witnessed. Casement's reports provoked a debate in Parliament. Newspapers across Europe began reporting the atrocities in the Congo. Stories emerged of mass murder, mass starvation, and epidemics of smallpox and other diseases the Europeans had brought. In all, ten million people died as a result of Leopold's tyrannical reign.

His response was to stage show trials of particularly brutal Belgian rubber agents. Their defense was that the natives were lazy and terror tactics were necessary to make them work. Most were acquitted and those found guilty escaped with light sentences.

The king of the Belgians seemed to be riding out the storm. But then the sixty-five-year-old Leopold became infatuated with a teenage mistress. This turned his people against him and made him a ridiculous figure in the eyes of the world, especially when he took her with him to Queen Victoria's funeral in London in 1901.

Social reformer Edmund Morel set up the Congo Reform Association with branches throughout Britain, and every Sunday members would be regaled with reports of atrocities from eye witnesses. Morel took his campaign to America, where Leopold paid lobbyists in Washington to defend his case. When one of these lobbyists was discovered trying to bribe members of Congress, however, atrocities in the Congo began to make the front pages.

To try to stem the tide of criticism, Leopold set up a new Commission of Enquiry with three judges—one Belgian, one Swiss, one Italian. Again he picked shrewdly. The judges knew no African languages, nor did they speak enough English to talk to the highly critical British and American missionaries who were leading the international campaign.

Nevertheless, the evidence they collected was so overwhelming it could not be ignored. They collected 370 depositions. One came from Chief Lontulu of Bolima, who had been flogged, held hostage, and set to work in chains. He laid on the table of the commission 110 twigs, one for each member of his tribe who had been murdered in the quest for rubber. He divided the twigs into four piles—one for tribal nobles, one for men, one for women, and one for children. Then he put a name to each of the twigs.

When government auditors examined the books, they discovered that the 32 million francs the government had lent Leopold were missing.

The testimony of Chief Lontulu and the other witnesses was so damning that the governor-general, the man nominally responsible for the system, committed suicide.

The commissioners returned to Europe and wrote their report. It was overwhelmingly negative. But Leopold still had one trick up his sleeve. The day before the report was published, every major newspaper in England received a document purporting to be a "complete and authentic résumé of the report." It came from the West African Missionary Association. The newspapers were delighted. Not only did it give them a one-day jump on the big story of the week, it was in English. Associated Press sent it on to America.

When the report itself came out, however, the papers realized that the summary was completely misleading. It was nowhere near as damning as the report itself. Worse, the West African Missionary Association did not actually exist: the "summary" had been delivered by a Belgian priest whose church had recently received a large donation by Leopold.

The full report detailed one atrocity after another—fatal beatings, random killings, senseless acts of cruelty.

The British and American governments began to put pressure on the Belgian government, but they did not control the Congo: it was Leopold's personal possession. When the Belgian government tried to buy it from him, and government auditors examined the books, they discovered that the 32 million francs the government had lent Leopold were missing. They suspected he had given the money to his teenage mistress. The money was written off along with 110 million francs worth of debt, much of it in the form of bonds given to Leopold's teenage mistress and the king's other lovers. And Leopold received another 100 million francs in compensation. But his atrocity-studded rule in the Congo was over. The Congo became part of Belgium in 1908. Leopold died the following year.

Mwanga II

When Mutesa I of Buganda—modern-day Uganda—died in 1884, he was succeeded by his son Mwanga, the first Ugandan Kabaka to take the throne without bloodshed.

This promising beginning was short-lived. While Mutesa had been erratic and two-faced, Mwanga II was brutal, sadistic, and paranoid, though crafty, with flashes of keen intelligence. Although initially favoring the Christians his father had encouraged, once he realized that their primary loyalty was to their God and not to him, he made an abrupt about-face, and by the end of the first year of his reign had brutally killed three Christians. Late in 1885 Mwanga had a visiting bishop assassinated at the border of his lands, perceiving the bishop to be a threat to his rule.

At this point Mwanga's madness and paranoia led him to become totally unhinged. He turned on the Christian communities, both Catholic and Protestant. In part his rage was brought to a head by the fact that many of his court pages had embraced the new faith, and as a result were resisting his amorous advances toward them. These young men became a special focus for his wrath, which soon became a full-blown persecution.

The witch hunt was carried out with an efficiency matched only by the courage of the victims. One eyewitness description of the arrest, trial, and execution of a man named Munyaga reads as follows: "Munyaga begged to be allowed to put on his *kansu* (white gown worn by Bugandan Christians), which they agreed to, and then they led him away." After a "cruel mockery of a trial," he was sentenced to death. On the same day, thirty-two other converts met the same fate.

When the executioner reported to Mwanga after the executions, and marveled that all the victims had gone to their deaths calling on God, Mwanga shrugged his shoulders and remarked that God could not have been paying much attention.

Mwanga went on to kill more than two hundred Christians while under the influence of hemp and home-fermented spirit. It was, as another eyewitness put it, "a martyrdom as terrible as any in Christian history." However, Mwanga's violent dementia finally proved to be his downfall.

When the rumor spread that all Christians and Muslims would be rounded up and executed, members of both faiths stormed Mwanga's palace and deposed him. Although Mwanga regained his throne, the British kept a careful watch over him, finally deposing him and exiling him in 1899 to the Seychelles, where he died.

Chronology

1868	Born H.H. Danieri Basamula-Ekkeri Mwanga II Mukasa.
1885	Has three Christians burnt alive.
1885	Orders the murder of a visiting bishop.
1886	Begins persecution of Christians on a grand scale.
1888	Deposed by combined Muslim and Christian rebels.
1889	Regains throne.
1897	Exiled by the British to the Seychelles.
1903	Dies.

Porfirio Díaz

Like many tyrants, Porfirio Díaz came to power in Mexico on the back of a democratic revolution, only to later turn into a repressive and violent dictator.

President Diaz, ex-soldier of the revolution and dictator of Mexico.

Born to a humble *mestizo* family in Mexico in 1830, Díaz studied to become a priest, but he abandoned the seminary to join the army at the outbreak of war with the United States in 1846. He went on to distinguish himself in the War of the Reform—a civil war—from 1857 to 1860, and in 1861 he was elected the federal representative from the state of Oaxaca.

In the struggle against the French between 1861 and 1867, he backed the liberals under Benito Juárez. His contribution was key to the collapse of the French-backed regime, which installed the Emperor Maximilian, and the establishment of a republic under Juárez. But when Juárez stood for re-election in 1871, Díaz led a rebellion, which failed. However, he defeated Juárez's successor Sebastian Lerdo de Tejada in the election of 1876. Falling from power in 1880, Díaz was re-elected in 1884 and held power until 1911.

Díaz' belief in economic growth at any price meant marginalizing the poor and expropriating the land of the Native American Indians. The result was the rise of groups of bandits. Díaz established the powerful state police force called the *rurales*, who terrorized Indian communities instead.

Díaz's economic miracle did not work. The aristocratic but democratically minded reformer Francisco Madero overthrew him in 1911. Díaz died on July 2, 1915 in exile in France.

Chronology

1830	Born September 15 in Oaxaca.
1846	Joins the army to fight the United States.
1857–60	Distinguishes himself in the War of the Reform.
1861–67	Helps overthrow the French-backed regime in Mexico.
1871	Stages abortive coup against Benito Juárez.
1876	Elected president.
1884–1910	Dispossesses the poor and terrorizes Indian communities.
1910	Fixes election.
1911	Overthrown by Francisco Madero in military coup.
1915	Dies July 2 in exile in Paris.

Cixi

Although Cixi started out as a lowly concubine, she ruled China for over fifty years. Her great beauty brought her to the attention of the Emperor Xianfeng, and she bore his only son, Tongzhi.

Dowager empress of China 1835–1908

When Emperor Xianfeng died, Tongzhi was only six years old, so Cixi ruled as regent, brutally suppressing the Taiping Rebellion in 1864 and the Nian Rebellion in 1868.

When Tongzhi came of age in 1873, Cixi refused to relinquish power. Two years later, he died—some say at his mother's hand. In violation of the laws of succession, Cixi placed Tongzhi's three-year-old cousin Guangxu on the throne, with herself as regent. Her full title was "Mother Auspicious Orthodox Heaven-Blessed Prosperous All-Nourishing Brightly-Manifest Calm Sedate Perfect Long-Lived Respectful Reverend Worshipful Illustrious Exalted Empress Dowager," but in the Forbidden City she was known as "The Old Buddha."

When Guangxu came of age in 1889, Tzu-hsi retired to a summer palace she had built with the money set aside to modernize the Chinese navy. But when Guangxu began instituting radical reforms, Cixi staged a coup, imprisoning the emperor in his palace while she ruled in his stead.

In 1900, she encouraged the Boxer Rebellion, which aimed to drive out all foreigners from China. When this was brutally put down by European troops, she fled Beijing and signed a humiliating peace treaty in 1902.

The day before Cixi died on November 15, 1908, Guangxu was killed in accordance with her deathbed wishes.

Chronology

1835	Born in obscurity.
1861	Becomes regent of China.
1875	Son dies in suspicious circumstances; becomes regent for 3-year-old cousin.
1889	Retires to summer palace.
1895	Imprisons emperor and seizes power.
1900	Encourages Boxer Rebellion: forced to flee when this fails.
1908	Dies November 15 after ordering murder of the emperor.

The funeral procession of Cixi, Dowager empress of China.

Kaiser Wilhelm II

Born with a withered left arm in Berlin in 1859, Wilhelm had a lifelong struggle to live up to the role of warrior king he believed the Prussian military state required of him.

The grandson of Queen Victoria, Wilhelm had a strict and authoritarian upbringing. He came to the throne on June 15, 1888 and quickly clashed with Otto von Bismarck, the "Iron Chancellor" responsible for the unification of Germany, forcing him to resign in 1890. Wilhelm wanted the world to know that he had absolute power in Germany, though he was utterly inept at using it, and he quickly alienated both Britain and Russia, even though both the future King George V of England and the Tsar were his cousins.

A militarist by upbringing and inclination, he believed in developing the strength of Germany's army and, encouraged by Admiral Alfred von Tirpitz, in 1900 he provided the money to build a German navy to rival the Royal Navy. During the Second Boer War (1899–1902), he supported the Boers against the British and later described Edward VII as "Satan." He made so many enemies that Germany risked being surrounded by hostile nations, inspiring his generals to develop the "Schlieffen Plan," a strategy that called for a lightning attack on France through Belgium, defeating any Western alliance before the Russians in the east could mobilize. However, a nervous breakdown in 1908 meant that Wilhelm had to relinquish some of the burdens of government.

When the Austrian Archduke Ferdinand was assassinated by a Serbian nationalist in Sarajevo in June 1914, Kaiser Wilhelm urged the Austro-Hungarian Empire to punish Serbia, failing to realize that a series of treaties among the European powers would mean that armed conflict between Austria and Serbia would engulf the whole of Europe in war. Even as the Kaiser tried to pull back from the consequences of his action, his army was putting the Schlieffen Plan into effect. The result was World War I and four years of pitiless slaughter.

During the war Wilhelm was commander-in-chief of the German armed forces, though he was largely a figurehead. He opposed the sacking of Erich Falkenhayn from his position of commander of land forces in 1916, but Paul von Hindenburg took over anyway. Facing defeat in 1918 the army turned against him, and when revolution engulfed Berlin he was forced to abdicate. His abdication proclamation read: "I herewith renounce for all time claims to the throne of Prussia and to the German Imperial throne connected therewith. At the same time I release all officials of the German Empire and of

Chronology

1859	Born January 27 in Potsdam near Berlin.
1887	Fails to renew treaty with Russia.
1888	Becomes Kaiser of Germany.
1890	Dismisses Bismarck.
1896	Sends telegram congratulating president of the Boers who were rebelling against British rule in South Africa.
1901	Tells British newspaper that most Germans are anti-English.
1904	Allows generals to develop the Schlieffen Plan.
1914	Pushes Austria-Hungary to punish Serbia, causing World War I.
1918	Flees to Holland.
1941	Dies June 4 in Doorn, Netherlands.

Prussia, as well as all officers, non-commissioned officers, and men of the navy and of the Prussian army, as well as the troops of the federated states of Germany, from the oath of fidelity which they tendered to me as their Emperor, King, and Commander-in-Chief. I expect of them that until the re-establishment of order in the German Empire they shall render assistance to those in actual power in Germany, in protecting the German people from the threatening dangers of anarchy, famine, and foreign rule. Proclaimed under our own hand and with the imperial seal attached. Signed Wilhelm, Amerongen, November 28, 1918."

He sought exile in Holland. The Dutch refused to extradite him to the Allies, who wanted to try him for starting the war. He spent his time writing two volumes of memoirs—*Memoirs 1878–1918* published in 1922 and *My Early Life* published in 1926.

With the rise of Hitler, Wilhelm sought to return to the throne. Hitler, however, had no time for him, even though Wilhelm supported the German nationalism and militarism that Hitler personified. Kaiser Wilhelm died in the Netherlands in 1941.

Kaiser Wilhelm II: the man, more than any other, responsible for World War I.

Juan Perón

Elected president of Argentina three times, Juan Perón died in office in 1974. The political movement that he founded is still active today as the Justicialist Party.

A career soldier, Juan Perón was Argentina's military attaché to Mussolini's Italy in the 1930s, where he got a master class in how to run a Fascist state. Returning to Argentina in 1941, he joined a plot that ousted the civilian government in 1943. He became secretary of labor and social welfare in the new military administration, giving him the opportunity to win the support of the *descamisados*—the "shirtless ones." He went on to become minister of war and vice-president.

In October 1945, another coup sought to oust the military government and Perón was arrested. But his beautiful mistress, the popular actress Eva Duarte, rallied the workers of Buenos Aires to demand his release. Freed,

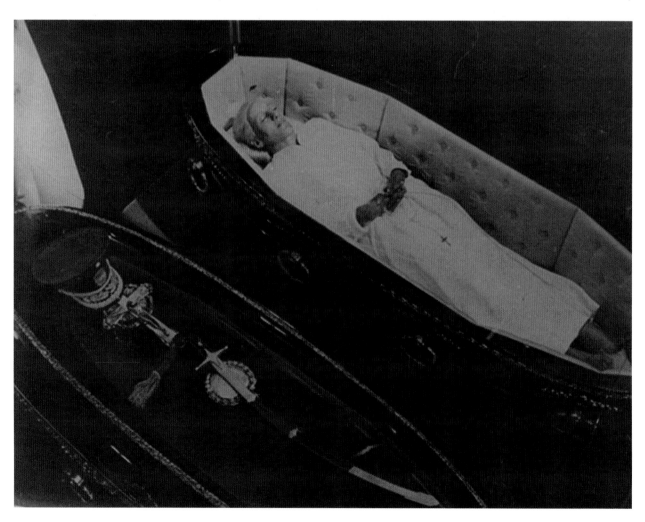

The coffins of Juan Perón and his first wife Eva Perón (1919–52), known as Evita, on public view at the Presidential Residence in Buenos Aires. The body of Eva Perón had been brought from a tomb in Italy.

Chronology

1895	Born October 8 in Buenos Aires province, Argentina.
1911	Enrols in military school.
1938	First wife dies; goes to Italy as military attaché.
1941	Returns to Argentina.
1943	Joins plot to oust civilian government.
1945	Military government overthrown; Perón arrested; Evita organizes rally to set him free; they marry.
1946	Elected president.
1951	Re-elected.
1952	Evita dies.
1955	Perón ousted; goes into exile in Spain.
1973	Returns to be elected president.
1974	Dies July 1 in Buenos Aires.
1976	Third wife Isabel ousted.

he made a speech to 300,000 people from the balcony of the presidential palace, promising peace, prosperity, and social justice. A few days later, he married Eva—or Evita, as she was known.

In February 1946, Perón was elected president. His popular appeal to the masses was augmented by the use of Fascist-style thugs to intimidate the opposition. Argentina had built up a large foreign-currency surplus from its exports to both sides during World War II and this money was utilized to fund development projects and benefits for the workers.

Politically, the regime was oppressive. In 1948, enemies including two priests were charged with plotting to assassinate Perón. When a judge refused to accept the government's flagrantly fraudulent evidence, he was removed from the bench.

Perón won a second election in 1951 with an increased majority. But Evita died of cancer the following year, plunging the country into mourning.

"I know that, like every woman of the people, I have more strength than I appear to have."

Eva Perón

Soon the money was running out and Perón's regime was engulfed by inflation and demagoguery. A coup ousted him in 1955 after it was revealed that, while petitioning the pope to beatify Evita, he had started a relationship with a new mistress.

In exile in Spain he managed to hold on to control of the Perónist movement by encouraging rivalry between competing factions. He married Isabel Martínez, an Argentine dancer, and the couple returned to Argentina in 1973 when elections were called. Perón won the presidency and insisted that his unpopular wife was named vice-president.

With the help of the army, he resumed his terror tactics, driving left-wingers to take up arms in a guerrilla war. Inflation soared once more. Perón died on July 1, 1974 and Isabel Perón became president. She became increasingly unpopular in the country, and on March 24, 1976 she was ousted and went into exile in Spain.

Josef Stalin

**Leader of
the USSR
1879–1953**

*Born Josef Vissarionovich Dzhugashvili, Stalin was beaten
savagely by his drunken father, who died when Josef was
just eleven.*

Josef Stalin was born in Georgia and did not start to learn Russian until
he went to school at the age of eight. When his father died, his doting
mother decided to have him groomed for the Orthodox priesthood. He was
sent to a seminary, where he earned the nickname Koba, after a famous
Georgian bandit and rebel, for his anti-tsarist views. He quit to become a
revolutionary organizer.

When the Social Democrats split in 1903, Koba joined the Bolshevik
faction under Lenin. He organized bank robberies to fund the party, joining
the Central Committee in 1912, and took the name Stalin, which translated
means "man of steel." He became the editor of the Bolshevik paper
Pravda—"Truth"—but was exiled to Siberia in 1913, returning to Petrograd
to play a key role in the Communist coup d'état in 1917.

When Lenin died in 1924, Stalin took over, ruthlessly crushing all
opposition. In 1928, he began an ambitious Five Year Plan to industrialize
Russia, funded by the export of grain, and continued the collectivization of
farming which resulted in famine, most notably in the Ukraine. Those who
resisted the regime in any way were executed, and a peasants' revolt was
savagely put down. It is estimated that twenty-five million people perished
as a result of collectivization.

In 1934, Stalin organized the murder of his colleague and potential
rival Sergey Kirov, and then used the assassination as a pretext for a purge.

Chronology

1879	Born December 21 in Gori, Georgia.	1939	Signs pact with Hitler; takes half of Poland; invades Finland.
1893	Attends seminary.		
1898	Begins anti-tsarist activities.	1941	Hitler attacks; Stalin prepares to flee; changes his mind at the last minute.
1899	Leaves seminary to become political organizer.		
		1941–45	Pours millions of men into the fight against the invading Germans.
1903	Joins Bolsheviks.		
1913–17	Exile in Siberia.	1945	Claims sole credit for victory over Hitler; imprisons returning prisoners of war.
1917	Plays prominent part in October Revolution.		
1924	Succeeds Lenin.	1946	Divides Europe with "Iron Curtain"; begins forcing repressive Communist regimes on Soviet hegemony.
1928–34	Forced collectivization kills 25 million.		
1934	Murders Sergey Kirov.		
1936–38	Purges party officials and army officers in show trials; secret police murder and imprison millions more.	1953	Uncovers "doctors' plot"; plans new purge, but dies suddenly on March 5, before any purge can be implemented.

Between 1936 and 1938, there was a series of show trials, with thousands of party officials and senior army officers found guilty of treason and executed. By 1939, of the 1,966 delegates to the 1934 party congress that had backed Kirov, 1,108 were dead; of the 139 members elected to the Central Committee that year, ninety-eight were dead. Meanwhile, Stalin's secret police chief Lavrenti Beria, a fellow Georgian, had arrested millions of ordinary people, executing, exiling, or imprisoning them in labor camps.

By 1939, there was no opposition in the Soviet Union, but the nation had been weakened by the extensive purges. Appalled, the Western nations refused to make any treaties with Stalin, leading him instead to sign a non-aggression pact with Hitler—even though the two were, at least in theory, sworn ideological enemies. Under a secret protocol, they divided Poland between them and Stalin invaded Finland, while Hilter took France and the Low Countries. But the non-aggression pact was a trick. Once Hitler felt secure in the West, he abrogated the agreement and on June 22, 1941, without warning, invaded the Soviet Union. The Red Army, purged of senior officers, could do little to resist. Thinking all was lost, Stalin was on the point of fleeing Moscow when, at the last minute, he changed his mind.

He took personal control of the army, appointing two brilliant commanders, Georgi Zhukov and Ivan Konev. With no regard for human life, Stalin threw millions of ill-equipped and poorly trained men into the fight, eventually turning the tide with sheer weight of numbers. Zhukov and Konev slowly and painfully fought their way through to Berlin and victory. Zhukov was rewarded with a distant posting in the east, while Konev remained abroad as commissar for Austria: nothing was to detract from Stalin's image as the hero who had won what the Soviets called "The Great Patriotic War."

Stalin forced repressive Communist regimes on the countries of eastern Europe and the Balkans that the Red Army had "liberated." Europe was divided in two by, in Winston Churchill's phrase, an "Iron Curtain" and hostility between East and West would develop into the Cold War.

Stalin seemed ready to begin a new round of purges of Kremlin doctors when, on March 5, 1953, he died of a brain hemorrhage.

Comrade Stalin lies in state in the Trade Union House, Moscow.

Benito Mussolini

**Dictator
of Italy
1883–1945**

Teacher-turned-socialist journalist, Benito Mussolini was wounded during World War I, when Italy fought against Germany on the side of the Allies.

Mussolini parades through the streets of Florence, May 1938, during a state visit from fellow dictator Adolf Hitler.

Having been expelled from the Socialist party for his support for the war, Mussolini started his own party called the Fasci di Combattimento—the "fasci" evoking the *fascae*, the bundle of rods with an ax-head protruding that was the symbol of authority in ancient Rome, and "combattimento" meaning struggle. Although this party was pro-labor and anti-Church, it was also fanatically nationalistic and sought to recreate the power of Italy in the days of the Roman Empire. Backed by industrialists and army officers, Mussolini organized teams of uniformed "Blackshirts" who fought other political parties on the streets.

On October 28, 1922, the Blackshirts marched on Rome. The government fell and Mussolini was given dictatorial powers by King Victor Emmanuel. He replaced the king's guard with his own *fascisti*, packed parliament with his own men, and set up a secret police force called the Ovra.

Although he famously got the trains to run on time and boosted industrial production by cutting taxes, he turned against labor, brutally repressing strikes. He seized Corfu from Greece and the port of Fiume, or Rijeka, from Yugoslavia.

In 1924 he held elections, the result of which had already been fixed. When the Socialist leader Giacomo Matteotti spoke out, he was found murdered. Mussolini responded to the resulting crisis by making Italy a one-party state with himself as "Il Duce"—"The Leader." Other political opponents were killed, trade unions were banned, and an accommodation was made with the Catholic Church.

Dreaming of a new Roman Empire, Mussolini invaded Abyssinia—modern Ethiopia—in 1935, gassing and bombing its defenseless inhabitants, and annexing the country in 1936 despite the condemnation of the—frankly toothless—League of Nations, the forerunner of the United Nations. He entered the so-called Pact of Steel with Hitler and gave military support to Franco and his Falangists in Spain.

In April 1939, Mussolini invaded Albania and in June 1940 joined World War II on Germany's side by attacking France. However, his military disasters in Greece and Libya forced Hitler to commit badly needed troops to the Balkans and North Africa.

Chronology	
1883	Born July 29 in Predappio, Italy.
1912	Becomes editor of socialist newspaper *Avanti!*
1914	Starts pro-war newspaper Il Popolo d'Italia; expelled from Socialist party.
1915	Joins Italian army as private.
1917	Wounded.
1918	Advocates the emergence of a dictator; hints that he might be the man.
1919	Begins the Fascist party Fasci di Combattimento.
1922	Marches on Rome; becomes Italy's youngest prime minister with dictatorial powers; seizes Corfu and Rijeka.
1924	Secures power with fraudulent election; murders opponents.
1929	Signs Lateran Treaty, guaranteeing pope's sovereignty in Vatican.
1935	Invades Abyssinia, gassing and bombing the populace.
1936	Annexes Abyssinia, announcing new Roman Empire; signs Pact of Steel with Hitler; sends troops to fight for Franco in Spain.
1939	Invades Albania.
1940	Joins war on Hitler's side; attacks France, Greece, and Egypt.
1943	Deposed and arrested; rescued by Germans; sets up new Fascist state in northern Italy; executes opponents.
1945	Flees for the border; captured; executed April 28 in Milan.

After Sicily fell to the Allies in July 1943, Mussolini was dismissed and arrested, and Italy changed sides. Imprisoned on September 12, Mussolini was rescued by a daring German commando raid, led by Hitler's super soldier, SS-Sturmbannführer Otto Skorzeny. With Hitler's backing he set up a new Fascist state in northern Italy, which was still under German occupation, and executed those who he felt had betrayed him—including his son-in-law Count Galeazzo Ciano.

The Allied drive up the Italian peninsula, however, was unstoppable, and, true to form, in April 1945 Mussolini and his mistress Clara Petacci fled. Captured by Italian partisans on the Austrian border, they were executed by firing squad and their bodies were hung upside down in the Piazza Loreto in Milan.

Adolf Hitler

Hitler is without doubt the most infamous tyrant of the twentieth century, possibly of all time. Dictator of Germany for twelve years, he ordered the imprisonment and death of well over six million people. He also provoked World War II, causing between thirty-five and sixty million more to die and Germany to be completely destroyed and dismembered.

Born and raised in Austria, the son of a customs officer who was brutal to his wife and children, Hitler idolized his mother and aspired to become an artist. Twice failing to gain admission to the Academy of Fine Arts in Vienna, he eked out a living painting postcards and advertisements. Lonely and isolated, he began to develop megalomaniacal fantasies and a hatred of Jews.

Hitler was rejected as unfit for service by the Austrian army but, on the outbreak of World War I, he was accepted by the 16th Bavarian Reserve Infantry Regiment. A brave, even reckless soldier, he was badly wounded in 1916 and gassed at the end of the war. Decorated four times, he won the Iron Cross First Class in 1918, although he was never promoted beyond the rank of corporal.

His time in the army turned him into a militaristic nationalist and he remained with his regiment until 1920, serving as an army political agent.

*Rabble-rouser:
on the eve of war
1939, Adolf Hitler
addresses the brown-
shirted masses.*

He left to work as head of the propaganda section of the German Workers' Party, which he had joined in 1919. He worked tirelessly for the party which, in August 1920, changed its name to the National-sozialistische Deutsche Arbeiterpartei—or Nazi Party.

Based in Munich, the party attracted former servicemen who felt that they had not lost the war on the battlefield but had been betrayed by Communists at home, among whom there were many Jewish intellectuals. Hitler also played on the discontent caused by the punitive nature of the Treaty of Versailles that had ended the war.

With the help of Ernst Röhm, an army staff officer, Hitler was elected president of the party in July 1921. In his hypnotic oratory, Hitler attacked Jews and Communists, while Röhm organized squads of storm troopers to protect party meetings and beat up political opponents. These thugs were organized into a private army called the Sturmabteilung, the SA, or Brownshirts.

Chronology

1889	Born April 20 in Braunau am Inn, Austria.		**1939**	Signs non-aggression pact with Stalin; invades Poland, forcing Britain and France to declare war.
1907	Moves to Vienna to become an artist.			
1913	Moves to Munich.			
1914	Joins German army.		**1940**	Overruns Scandinavia, the Low Countries, and France; defeated by the Royal Air Force in the Battle of Britain.
1916	Seriously wounded on Western Front.			
1918	Gassed; awarded Iron Cross First Class.			
1919	Joins German Workers' Party.		**1941**	Overruns the Balkans and Greece; invades the Soviet Union; declares war on the United States.
1921	Becomes president of Nazi Party.			
1923	Attempted putsch fails; jailed for treason; writes *Mein Kampf.*			
1932	Nazis become largest party in Reichstag.		**1942**	Defeated by the British at El Alamein. The "Final Solution"—with Hitler's approval—is put into operation following the Wannsee Conference in Berlin.
1933	Appointed Reich chancellor; jails Communists; takes dictator powers.			
1934	Purges party in the Night of the Long Knives; takes over presidency, naming himself Führer of the Third Reich.		**1943**	Defeated by the Russians at Stalingrad; driven out of North Africa by the Allies, who invade Italy.
1935	Strips Jews of citizenship; starts re-arming.		**1944**	Allies land in Normandy; bomb attempt on Hitler's life fails; short-lived counter-offensive in the Ardennes.
1936	Sends troops into the Rhineland; forms Axis with Italy; signs pact with Japan.			
1938	Annexes Austria; takes over Sudetenland after being appeased at Munich Conference; overruns western Czechoslovakia.		**1945**	Germany invaded by Allies; Hitler commits suicide with Eva Braun in Berlin bunker on April 30.

In November 1923, Hitler staged the Munich Beer Hall Putsch, a failed attempt to take over the Bavarian government. Convicted of treason, he was sentenced to five years' imprisonment. In Landsberg prison, he wrote *Mein Kampf*—"My Struggle"—in which he outlined his political philosophy. He extolled the virtues of racial purity and the force of the will, and declared his unending opposition to Jews, Communists, liberals, and foreign capitalists. Germany, he said, would rise to become the world's dominant power. It would take its revenge for its defeat in World War I, unite the German-speaking peoples now living in other countries, and expand to the east, finding Lebensraum, or "living space," in central Europe and Russia. It was a philosophy of tyranny.

Released after nine months, Hitler recruited Herman Göring, Heinrich Himmler, and master propagandist Josef Goebbels to the cause. The worldwide economic collapse of 1929 brought chaos to the streets that could be exploited by the Nazi storm troopers. Hitler also forged an alliance with the Nationalist Party, led by industrialist Alfred Hugenberg, increasing Nazi representation in the German parliament—the Reichstag—from twelve to 107.

In the 1932 elections, representation increased to 230, making the Nazis the biggest party in the Reichstag and, in January 1933, the German president—the aging war hero Paul von Hindenberg—finally agreed to appoint Hitler Reich chancellor.

"How fortunate for governments that the people they administer don't think."

Adolf Hitler

Adolf Hitler

When the Reichstag was burned down in February 1933—in a fire possibly started by the Nazis themselves—Hitler found an excuse to outlaw the Communist Party and arrest its leaders. In March 1933, an Enabling Act gave Hitler dictatorial powers for four years. He used this to dismantle all other political parties, purge the government of Jews, and bring all its offices under direct control of the Nazi Party. Then on June 30, 1934—the Night of the Long Knives—he purged the party of radicals, murdering Röhm and hundreds of others who posed a threat to Hitler's domination. The SA were replaced by the Schutzstaffel or SS under Himmler who were loyal only to Hitler himself, and a secret police force called the Gestapo was set up.

When Hindenberg died in August 1934, Hitler took over the presidency, naming himself Führer of the Nazi state he now dubbed the Third Reich. He sent Jews, political enemies, and anyone else he found "undesirable" to concentration camps set up by the SS. In 1935, the Nuremberg Racial Laws stripped Jews of citizenship and, in defiance of the Versailles Treaty, Hitler set up an air force (the Luftwaffe), started building tanks, and sent troops into the demilitarized Rhineland.

In 1936, he formed the Rome-Berlin "Axis" with Italy's Fascist dictator Benito Mussolini, and signed an anti-Communist pact with Japan. In 1938, he annexed Austria and demanded that Czechoslovakia hand over the Sudetenland, a border region where the inhabitants spoke German. Unprepared for war, the Western allies sought to appease Hitler, and Britain and France agreed to the dismemberment of Czechoslovakia at the Munich Conference in September 1938. However, Hitler—not content with the Sudetenland—quickly swallowed up the rest of Czechoslovakia and began making yet more territorial demands.

The gates of Auschwitz concentration camp, where over a million people were killed.

After concluding a nonaggression pact with the Soviet Union on August 23, 1939, Hitler invaded Poland on September 1. Britain and France declared war, but there was little they could do. Poland was quickly overrun, with the eastern half being taken by the Soviet Union. Hitler then seized Denmark and Norway.

Hitler's fast-moving mechanized forces overran the Low Countries and France in a matter of weeks, but his plans to invade the United Kingdom had to be shelved when the Luftwaffe failed to gain control of the skies in the Battle of Britain.

In April 1941, he invaded Yugoslavia and Greece and, in June, he tore up the nonaggression pact and invaded the Soviet Union. Although his army won spectacular victories in the field, they failed to take Moscow before the Russian winter set in. The Russians began to exact a huge toll on the German armies, and in the winter of 1942–43 defeated the Germans at Stalingrad. Meanwhile, Britain had beaten decisively Hitler's seemingly invincible mechanized forces in the deserts of North Africa.

Hitler now had another powerful enemy to face. In December 1941, the Japanese had attacked the U.S. Pacific Fleet at its base in Pearl Harbor, Hawaii, beginning a war in the Pacific. Hitler promptly declared war on the United States.

"Any alliance whose purpose is not the intention to wage war is senseless and useless."

Adolf Hitler

At home, Hitler's pathological hatred of Jews resulted in the "Final Solution." In the Holocaust, six million Jews—along with gypsies, homosexuals, Slavs, and other people thought to be inferior—were murdered in death camps, worked to death in labor camps, or simply died from maltreatment and disease.

By 1943, the war had turned against Hitler. On the Eastern Front, the Soviet army was pushing the Germans out of Russia. Sicily had been invaded, Mussolini had fallen, Allied forces were pushing their way up the Italian peninsula, and British and American bombers were pounding German cities every night.

On June 6, 1944, Allied troops landed on the coast of Normandy. Hitler had now taken the conduct of the war into his own hands and persisted in making disastrous military blunders. A plot was hatched among a number of his senior officers and on July 20, 1944 a bomb went off under a table where he was working. It failed to kill him. Those responsible were rounded up, tortured, and executed horribly.

In December 1944, Hitler staged a short-lived counter-offensive in the Ardennes. But he no longer had the manpower or the industrial might to resist the forces set against him. As the Russians and the Allies closed in on Berlin, Hitler organized a defense to the last man. Germany, he believed, deserved to be destroyed because it had failed to live up to his great vision for it. However, his courage failed him. On April 29, 1945, he married his long-term mistress Eva Braun, and the following day the two of them committed suicide. In accordance with Hitler's instructions, their bodies were burned.

Francisco Franco

Dictator
of Spain
1892–1975

An ardent royalist, Francisco Paulino Hermenegildo Teódulo Franco y Bahamonde Salgardo Pardo was shocked when Spain became a republic in 1931 and the king was forced to leave. Already the youngest general in the army, he rose to become chief of the general staff despite his monarchist views.

When the left-wing Popular Front won the election in February 1936, Francisco Franco was exiled to the Canary Islands. From there he organized a Nationalist conspiracy that led to the outbreak of the Spanish Civil War. On July 17, 1936, garrisons across Spain revolted and Franco's nationalists took control of Morocco, then a Spanish colony, the Balearic Islands with the exception of Minorca, and much of northern Spain.

Franco flew to Morocco and airlifted the large garrison of Spanish Foreign Legion troops stationed there to mainland Spain and marched on Madrid, which they besieged. On September 29, 1936, the Nationalists established their own government at Burgos, with Franco at its head. The following year, he became head of the Nationalist Falange Party.

With the aid of the Nazi German Legion Kondor and Fascist Italy's Corpo Truppe Volontgari, he ground down the Loyalists, who were backed by the Soviet Union, France, Mexico, and a volunteer International Brigade. There were atrocities on both sides. It is estimated that more than fifty thousand were executed, murdered, or assassinated. The Germans used the war to try out new tactics that they would employ during World War II, most notably carpet bombing the undefended Basque market town of Guernica.

By February 1939, nearly half-a-million Spaniards had fled across the border into France. The Republican government fled into exile on March 5. Two days later fighting broke out between Communist and non-Communist forces in Madrid. Franco moved in for the kill. Madrid fell to the Nationalists on March 28, 1939 and the Republican forces disbanded. It is estimated that half-a-million were killed in the Spanish Civil War, with another half-a-million dead from starvation and disease.

With the end of the Civil War, Franco became dictator of Spain. He outlawed all opposition parties and imprisoned and executed thousands

Franco meets Adolf Hitler, October 23, 1940. Despite his support for Hitler, Franco declined to offer any practical help.

of Loyalists. However, he managed to keep Spain out of World War II, though he did send workers to aid industrial production in Germany and the Spanish volunteer División Azul, or Blue Brigade, fought on the Russian Front. He also provided facilities for German ships.

Lacking any strong ideology, Franco sought support from the royalist Carlists, the National Syndicalists, and the National Catholic Party. These were combined in a single ruling coalition called the Movimiento Nacional, which was so heterogeneous that it lacked the strict ideology of the German Nazi Party or the Italian Fascists. It was a conservative, traditionalist, rightist regime that emphasized order and stability, rather than a social or political vision.

Although he was a monarchist, Franco left the throne vacant and usurped royal powers. He wore the uniform of a captain general, a rank traditionally reserved for the king in Spain. He lived in the Prado Palace and adopted the kingly privilege of walking beneath a canopy.

His official titles were Jefe del Estado (Chief of State) and Generalísimo de los Ejércitos Españoles (Highest General of the Spanish Armed Forces). But he also took as his personal title por la gracia de Dios, Caudillo de España y de la Cruzada, or "by the grace of God, Caudillo of Spain and of the Crusade"—"by the grace of God" is legal phraseology only used by monarchs.

During his rule, nongovernment trade unions and all opposition political parties—including Communists, anarchists, liberal democrats, and Basque and Catalan nationalists—were suppressed. Freemasons were also outlawed as Franco believed they were conspiring against him.

After World War II, Franco made a show of liberal reforms, introducing a bill of rights and promising to restore the monarchy. During the Cold War his anti-Communist stance made him an ally of the United States. In 1953, an alliance was concluded that allowed the United States to establish air bases on Spanish territory, and in 1955, with North American backing, Spain was admitted to the United Nations.

During the 1960s, Franco reversed many of his liberal stances, repressing unrest among the Basques, workers, students, and the clergy. In July 1969, he chose Juan Carlos de Bourbon, grandson of the previous king, as heir to the throne, who succeeded when Franco died in 1975.

Chronology

1892	Born December 4 in El Ferrol, Spain.
1907	Enrols in military academy.
1912	Fights in war in Morocco.
1920	Appointed deputy commander of Spanish Foreign Legion in Morocco.
1921–26	Fights in Riff Rebellion.
1923	Promoted commander of the Foreign Legion.
1926	Becomes Spain's youngest brigadier general.
1928	Appointed director of the military academy.
1934	Suppresses miners' revolt, earning respect of right, hatred of left.
1935	Named chief of the general staff.
1936	Exiled to Canaries; returns with Foreign Legion; establishes Nationalist government with himself at its head.
1937	Becomes leader of ruling Falange Party.
1939	Defeats Loyalists, imprisoning and executing thousands.
1947	Promises return of monarchy.
1953	Allows United States to establish military bases in Spain.
1969	Names Juan Carlos as heir to the throne.
1975	Dies November 20 in Madrid.

Although he was a monarchist, Franco left the throne vacant and usurped royal powers.

Fulgencio Batista y Zaldívar

**Dictator
of Cuba
1901–1973**

Fulgencio Batista y Zaldívar is now best known for the fact that he was deposed by the young revolutionary Fidel Castro, who went on to become a tyrant himself.

Batista, accompanied by U.S. Army General Malin Craig, arrives in Washington, 1938.

Born January 16, 1901, the son of an impoverished farmer, Batista joined the army in 1921. In September 1933 he organized the "sergeants' revolt" which toppled the provisional Cuban government of Carlos Manuel de Cespedes who had replaced the previous dictator Gerardo Machado y Morales. Rather than taking power himself, Batista controlled a series of civilian puppet presidents while pulling the strings in the background as army chief of staff until 1940, when he was elected president.

He began a huge program of public works and greatly expanded the economy—allowing the Mafia, under New York gangster Meyer Lansky, to run the casinos there. Under Lansky's criminal guidance, Cuba became a resort island for the United States, famed for its music, cigars, and rum. In 1944, the wealthy Batista retired to Florida only to return to Cuba in 1952, seizing power in a bloodless coup. Re-elected in 1958, his second period in office was marked by brutal repression. He controlled the press, the universities, and the Congress with an iron fist, while embezzling huge sums of money.

The widespread corruption led to the growth of a guerrilla movement under Fidel Castro. Batista's flagrant abuse of power led U.S. President Eisenhower to ban the sale of arms to Cuba. Without American backing, Batista could not resist Castro's forces and on January 1, 1959 he fled to the Dominican Republic. He lived comfortably in exile on the island of Madeira and in Estoril, near Lisbon, dying in Marbella, Spain, on August 6, 1973.

Chronology

1901	Born January 16 in Banes, Cuba.
1921	Joins the Cuban army.
1933	Stages "sergeants' revolt."
1940	Elected president.
1944	Retires to Florida a wealthy man.
1952	Returns to power in Cuba after bloodless coup.
1958	Castro's guerrillas make first significant gains.
1959	Batista flees into exile.
1973	Dies August 6 in Spain.

Achmed Sukarno

Achmed Sukarno came to prominence in 1930s' Indonesia as a nationalist politician seeking independence from the Netherlands. As a result, he spent two years in a Dutch prison and eight in exile.

President of Indonesia 1901–1970

When the Japanese invaded during World War II, Achmed Sukarno welcomed them as liberators, acting as their chief adviser and supplying labor, soldiers, and women for them.

At the end of the war, Sukarno was persuaded to declare Indonesia's independence. The Dutch were finally forced to concede sovereignty in 1949 and Sukarno quickly established himself in the governor-general's lavish palace.

He easily won the first presidential election, but his government was notoriously corrupt. After extracting a billion dollars worth of aid from the United States, he switched sides in the Cold War and took a billion dollars from the Soviet Union. Meanwhile inflation soared. In 1959 he dissolved parliament and in 1963 made himself president for life.

He became increasingly fearful of a military coup and in 1965 he approved a Communist-backed plot to kidnap six top army generals who were then brutally murdered. General Suharto, commander of the Jakarta garrison, reacted by slaughtering more than 300,000 Communist suspects. Suharto gradually took over power, forcing Sukarno to retire in 1968, and installed himself as president.

Chronology

1901	Born June 6 in Surabaja, Java.
1928	Founds Indonesian Nationalist Party.
1942	Welcomes Japanese invaders, becoming chief collaborator.
1945	Declares independence.
1949	Dutch cede sovereignty; Sukarno takes power.
1959	Dissolves parliament.
1963	Declares himself president for life.
1965	Implicated in coup against the army.
1966	Cedes wide powers to Suharto.
1968	Stands down as president.
1970	Dies of kidney failure June 21 in Jakarta, Indonesia.

Sukarno on an official state visit to Kuwait in 1962.

François Duvalier ("Papa Doc")

President
of Haiti
1907–1971

Around thirty thousand Haitians are believed to have been killed as a result of François Duvalier's repressive regime. Reviving Haiti's voodoo traditions, he built up a personality cult around himself, often wearing dark glasses and basing his image on the voodoo spirit Baron Samedi to inspire fear and respect.

François Duvalier earned his nickname "Papa Doc" when he worked as a rural physician tirelessly fighting to eradicate malaria and yaws during an epidemic in Haiti in the 1940s. At the same time he became involved in a writers' group that explored black nationalism and voodoo.

After serving as minister of health, François Duvalier became president in a fixed election in 1957, ostensibly winning the biggest majority in Haitian history. He then set about consolidating his power, employing a ruthless group of thugs called the "Tontons Macoutes"—or "Bogeymen"— to terrorize the populace and assassinate suspected opponents of the regime.

"I accept the people's will. As a revolutionary, I have no right to disregard the will of the people."

François "Papa Doc" Duvalier

After his chief aide, Clément Barbot, deputized for him when he suffered a heart attack, Duvalier had him imprisoned then murdered. Then the United States withdrew its aid after Duvalier had his term of office illegally extended. In 1964, he was declared president for life. Haiti was shunned by other nations and Duvalier was excommunicated from the Catholic Church in 1966 for harassing the clergy. But he managed to hold on to power using a mixture of voodoo

Chronology

1907	Born April 14 in Port-au-Prince, Haiti.
1934	Graduates from University of Haiti School of Medicine.
1943	Joins U.S.-backed anti-yaws campaign.
1946	Heads National Public Heath Service.
1949	Becomes minister of health.
1957	Elected president in fraudulent election.
1959	Imprisons deputy, later murdering him.
1961	Fixes legislative elections; extends term of office; loses U.S. aid.
1963	Begins cult of personality.
1964	Becomes president for life.
1966	Excommunicated for harassing clergy.
1971	Dies April 21, Port-au-Prince.
1986	Son Baby Doc flees into exile.

and strong-arm gangster tactics, always keeping a pearl-handled pistol, loaded, on his desk in the presidential palace.

When Duvalier died in 1971, he was succeeded by his nineteen-year-old son Jean-Claude "Baby Doc" Duvalier. The United States put pressure on Baby Doc to soften the tyrannical regime instigated by his father, but the corruption was endemic and the Tontons Macoutes would not change their ways. Popular protest turned into open rebellion in November 1985. On February 7, 1986, a U.S. Air Force jet carried Baby Doc and his wife into exile in France.

Aging and ill, Papa Doc Duvalier faces the camera shortly after his 1966 excommunication.

Enver Hoxha

*With the aid of the Sigurimi, the feared Albanian secret police,
Hoxha maintained his forty-year term in power through the ruthless
imprisonment and execution of anyone who opposed him.*

Born to a Muslim family in southern Albania, Enver Hoxha won a
scholarship to study in France, where he became a Communist. He had
returned to Albania when his country was invaded by the Italians in 1939
and set up a tobacco shop in the capital, Tirana, which became a front for
the resistance.

When the Communist Party of Albania was formed in 1941, he became
general secretary and political commissar of the Communist-dominated
Army of National Liberation. When the Germans left in 1944, he set up a
provisional government and began trials of those accused of collaborating.
Those found guilty were executed, ridding him of a number of political
enemies. And when Yugoslavia broke with the Soviet Union in 1948,
Hoxha purged the party of pro-Tito Communists.

A Stalinist, Hoxha fell out with Stalin's successor Khrushchev and
aligned Albania with China. At home, he confiscated private property and
closed churches and mosques. He herded the people into collective farms
and newly built factories. Anyone who resisted was exiled, imprisoned, or
shot. Even so, his efforts to develop the country failed.

Relations with China eventually soured and Chinese aid to Albania
was cut off in 1978. Now an international pariah, Hoxha declared that
Albania would become a socialist paradise on its own. In 1981, to ensure
the succession of a younger generation of Communists, he ordered the
execution of a number of government and party leaders. He died in 1985
after forty years in power. Soon after, the Communist Party itself was ousted.

Chronology

1908	Born October 16 in Gjirokastër, Albania.
1930	Goes to France to study engineering.
1934	Serves as secretary in Albanian consulate in Brussels.
1936	Returns to Albania to become a teacher.
1939	Dismissed for refusing to join Albanian Fascist Party; opens tobacconist's shop.
1941	Founds Albanian Communist Party; becomes general secretary.
1944	Heads up provisional government; starts show trials.
1948	Purges party of Titoists; closes churches and confiscates property.
1961	Breaks with Soviet Union.
1978	Breaks with China.
1981	Culls party and government leaders.
1985	Dies April 11 in Tirana.

Kim Il-sung

Originally named Kim Song Ju, the young Kim fled with his parents to Manchuria in 1925 to escape the harsh Japanese occupation of Korea. When he returned, he went on to become Korean premier.

Leader of North Korea 1912–1994

Kim joined the Communist Party, taking the name of an earlier legendary guerrilla fighter against the Japanese as his nom de guerre.

With the Japanese surrender in 1945, Korea was split in two with a U.S.-backed government in the south and Kim's Soviet-backed government in the north. In 1950, Kim sought to unify the country by force, precipitating the Korean War. He was initially successful, but a U.S.-led United Nations force overran the north and Kim's Communist state was only saved by the intervention of the Chinese.

After the ceasefire in 1953, Kim began a purge of internal opposition, murdering rivals for power. He instigated a cult of personality, calling himself the "Great Leader" and filling the country with his portraits and statues. The people were forced into factories and collective farms.

When Kim Il-sung died in 1994, his son Kim Jong-il took over as "Dear Leader." Although famine ravaged his hardline state, Kim Jong-il kept North Korea's borders closed and maintained a huge military and nuclear weapons program. On his death in 2011, he was succeeded by his son Kim Jong-un, who was proclaimed the "Eternal General Secretary of the Workers' Party."

Chronology

1912	Born April 15 in Man'gyondae near P'yongyang, Korea.
1925	Flees to Manchuria with family.
1945	Korea divided.
1948	Becomes premier of newly created Democratic People's Republic of Korea.
1950	Begins Korean War.
1953	With cease-fire, begins elimination of internal opposition.
1967	Purges party with help of Kim Jong-il.
1972	Becomes president of North Korea.
1994	Dies July 8 in P'yongyang; succeeded by son, Kim Jong-il.

Kim Il-sung, last of the Stalinists. Thanks to his policies, North Korea has suffered famine after famine.

Augusto Pinochet

President
of Chile
1915–2006

After seizing power in a bloody CIA-backed coup, General Augusto Pinochet ruled Chile with a rod of iron for two decades, during which time human rights violations became the norm of Chilean life.

Hailing from an upper middle-class background, Augusto Pinochet entered the military academy in Santiago at the age of eighteen, graduating three years later as a second lieutenant. By 1968 he had risen to the rank of brigadier general.

In 1970, Salvador Allende, a Marxist, became president of Chile with the backing of the Christian Democrats, and began restructuring Chilean society along socialist lines. In the process he expropriated the U.S.-owned copper-mining companies, alienating the U.S. government and foreign investors. He further annoyed Washington by establishing relations with Cuba and Communist China, which the United States did not recognize at that time. As a result, the United States imposed tough economic sanctions and the CIA spent millions of dollars destabilizing the Allende regime, much of it going into Pinochet's pockets.

By 1972, the Chilean economy had collapsed. With no foreign investment, production had come to a standstill. There were widespread strikes, runaway inflation, food shortages, and civil unrest. With the backing of the armed forces, Pinochet staged a military coup on September 11, 1973. The coup was bloody even by Latin American standards. The navy seized the key port of Valparaíso, while the army surrounded the presidential palace in Santiago. Allende refused to step down. When the palace was overrun a few hours later, he was found dead. It appears that he shot himself rather than face inevitable torture and execution.

Chronology

1915	Born November 25 in Valparaíso, Chile.
1936	Graduates from military academy.
1973	Stages coup against the elected government of Salvador Allende.
1974	Assumes sole power.
1978	His murderous rule endorsed by 75 percent vote in plebiscite.
1981	Introduces new constitution that guarantees his presidency for a further eight years.
1988	Rejected by a vote of 55 percent to 43 percent.
1990	Steps down.
1998	Arrested in London for murder.
2000	Returned to Chile a free man.
2006	Dies January 10 in Santiago.

A junta took over and declared martial law. Those who violated the curfew were shot on sight. Pinochet was named president two days later. He broke off relations with Cuba—the U.S. president Richard Nixon had staged his famous rapprochement with China by then—and moved against Allende's supporters.

Some fourteen thousand would be tried and executed or expelled from the country, while Pinochet claimed he was only trying to "restore institutional normality" to Chile.

In June 1974 Pinochet assumed sole power, with the rest of the junta relegated to an advisory role. Under Pinochet's tyrannical rule, it is estimated that twenty thousand people were killed and torture was widespread.

While Pinochet continued to maintain tight control over the political opposition, he was rejected by a plebiscite in 1988. He eventually stepped down in 1990 after securing immunity from prosecution in Chile. He stayed on as army chief of staff. However, during a shopping trip to London in October 1998, he was arrested on a Spanish warrant charging him with murder. He was later accused of torture and human rights violations. For sixteen months, he fought his extradition through the British courts. In January 2000, the British Home Secretary Jack Straw decided Pinochet was too ill to stand trial and sent him back to Chile. He died in 2006.

Pinochet was visited by former Prime Minister Margaret Thatcher while under house arrest in England.

"I regret and suffer those losses, but it's God's will. He will pardon me if I committed excesses, but I don't think I did."

General Augusto Pinochet

Ferdinand Marcos

A trained lawyer, Ferdinand Marcos was convicted of assassinating a political opponent of his father in 1939 and, from his condemned cell, argued his case up to the Philippine Surpreme Court, where he won an acquittal.

During World War II Ferdinand Marcos collaborated with the Japanese who occupied the Philippines—though he later claimed to have led the Filipino resistance, a fiction in which the United States colluded, awarding him medals. He emerged from the war a wealthy man and served in the Philippine house of representatives and the senate, switching parties when it suited him.

Ferdinand Marcos raises a victory salute. Imelda sits beside him.

Chronology

1917	Born September 11 in Sarrat, Philippines.
1939	Found guilty of murder.
1940	Acquitted by Supreme Court.
1942–45	Collaborates with Japanese during World War II.
1946–47	Assistant to president of the Philippines.
1949–59	Serves in house of representatives.
1959–65	Serves in senate; senate president 1963.
1965	Changes party to win nomination; elected president; supports United States in Vietnam war.
1972	Declares martial law; imprisons political opponents.
1981	Suspends martial law, but rules by decree.
1983	Opposition leader Benigno Aquino killed on Imelda's orders.
1986	"Wins" election by huge voting fraud; goes into exile in Hawaii.
1989	Dies September 28 in Honolulu.
1993	Imelda convicted of corruption by Philippine court.

Elected president in 1965, he won a second term in 1969. But in 1972, he declared martial law, imprisoned his political opponents, dissolved congress, suspended habeas corpus, and used the army as his private police force. He then wrote a new constitution giving himself considerably more power. His wife, Imelda, and other family members were given lucrative government posts. While the Filipino people lived in abject poverty, the Marcoses flaunted their extravagant lifestyle, Imelda becoming world-renowned for her huge collection of shoes.

In 1981, Marcos ended martial law, but continued to rule by decree. Opposition leader Benigno Aquino, who had gone into exile after being imprisoned for eight years by Marcos, returned in 1983, but was shot dead on the orders of Imelda in front of a plane full of journalists after he had landed at Manila. This sparked riots. An official enquiry blamed a high-ranking general, Fabian Ver. A family friend of the Marcoses, Ver was acquitted when the case went to court.

To reassert his authority, Marcos held an election. Benigno Aquino's widow Corazon ran against him. Marcos was declared the winner, but only after thirty election officials walked out in protest at voting fraud. Marcos quickly arrested his opponents, provoking more rioting as Aquino was widely thought to have won the election. On February 25, 1986, both Marcos and Aquino were inaugurated in competing ceremonies. The following evening Marcos accepted the United States' offer to fly him and his wife to exile in Hawaii.

After they were gone, it was discovered that they had embezzled millions of dollars. But Marcos was deemed too ill to stand trial and died on September 28, 1989. Imelda was acquitted of racketeering by a U.S. federal court in 1990, and returned to the Philippines in 1991. She went back into politics and stood for election. She served in congress from 1995 to 1998.

Nicolae Ceausescu

Dictator of Romania 1918–1989

Nicolae Ceausescu fostered a pervasive personality cult around himself and was the hardline Communist leader of Romania. His tyrannical rule kept the country in poverty for twenty-five years.

Ceausescu became a Communist at the age of eighteen. During World War II, he was imprisoned with the influential Communist leader Gheorghe Gheorghiu-Dej, while his wife Elena, also a professed Communist, openly fraternized with Nazi officers.

When the Red Army entered Romania in 1944, Ceausescu became secretary of the Union of Communist Youth. Shortly after a Communist government was installed in 1947, he became minister of agriculture.

In 1950, he became deputy minister of defense and took the rank of major general. When Gheorghiu-Dej consolidated his power in 1952, Ceausescu was brought onto the Central Commitee, eventually becoming his deputy. Succeeding Gheorghiu-Dej in 1965, he became first secretary of the Communist Party, then general secretary of the Communist Party. In 1967 he became president of the state council and head of state as well.

In foreign policy Ceausescu kept his distance from Moscow. Domestically his regime was as oppressive as any in the Soviet bloc. His feared secret police, the Securitate, stamped out any opposition and maintained ruthless control of the press and the media. Like the Soviet Union in the 1930s, Ceausescu embarked on a crash program of industrialization, which built up massive foreign debts. To pay these off, he exported most of Romania's food supply: the result—famine.

He also oversaw a massive building program, which demolished ancient Romanian villages and replaced them with soulless Soviet-style apartment blocks. Large areas of the Romanian capital Bucharest were demolished to build luxurious palaces for the Ceausescus.

Chronology

1918	Born January 26, at Scornicesti, Romania.
1936	Joins Communist Party.
1939	Marries Elena Petrescu.
1940	Imprisoned for Communist activities.
1944	Becomes secretary of the Union of Communist Youth.
1948	Becomes minister of agriculture.
1950	Becomes deputy minister of defense.
1952	Becomes deputy leader of Communist Party.
1965	Becomes first secretary, then general secretary of Communist Party.
1967	Becomes president of the state council and head of state.
1974	Takes newly created post of president of Romania.
1982	Export drive to pay off foreign debt causes famine.
1989	Falls from power; convicted of mass murder and shot.

To pay off massive foreign debts, he exported most of Romania's food supply: the result—famine.

Meanwhile, the impoverished Romanians had to suffer a megalomaniacal cult of personality surrounding Ceausescu and his wife. Family members were given lucrative government posts and their loathsome son Nicu, who had a serious drinking problem, scandalized Bucharest with his atrocious behavior and gambling away vast sums.

Despite ruthless oppression, opposition grew. On December 17, 1989, Ceausescu ordered his secret police to fire on antigovernment demonstrators in the city of Timisoara. Far from quelling opposition, demonstrations quickly spread to Bucharest and Ceausescu found himself shouted down while making a speech—something that had simply never happened before.

On December 22 the Romanian army deserted him and sided with the demonstrators. Ceausescu and his wife tried to flee the capital in a helicopter but were captured. On December 25 they were tried by a military tribunal, convicted of mass murder and other crimes, and shot by a firing squad. Four days later Romania ceased to be a Communist state and five months after that the first free elections for over fifty years were held.

Nicolae Ceausescu addresses his puppet parliament, circa 1985.

Jean-Bédel Bokassa

President of the Central African Republic 1921–1996

Emulating his hero, Napoléon Bonaparte, Jean-Bédel had himself crowned Emperor Bokassa I in a grandiose ceremony costing a third of his country's annual budget. Narcissistic and a brutal despot, Bokassa tortured and killed his rivals with impunity.

Born in French Equatorial Africa, the son of a village chief, Jean-Bédel Bokassa was orphaned at the age of twelve. Educated in mission schools, he joined the French colonial army in 1939 as a private. He distinguished himself in the war in Indochina, winning medals and eventually rising to the rank of captain.

When French Equatorial Africa gained its independence as the Central African Republic in 1960, the new president David Dacko invited Bokassa to head the armed forces. In 1966, Bokassa used his position to oust Dacko and declared himself president.

He began a reign of terror, taking all important government posts for himself. He personally supervised judicial beatings and ordered amputations for theft.

In 1977, in emulation of his hero Napoleon, he crowned himself emperor of the Central African Empire in a ceremony costing $200 million, practically bankrupting the country. His diamond-encrusted crown alone cost $5 million. Bokassa already had a notorious reputation abroad, and no foreign leaders attended the coronation.

Bokassa's rule then became even more tyrannical. In 1979, he

Jean-Bedel Bokassa with the Romanian dictator, Nicolae Ceausescu, in 1970.

Bokassa during his coronation in 1977, seated on a somewhat gaudy throne.

had hundreds of schoolchildren arrested for refusing to wear the expensive uniforms made in a factory he owned. He personally supervised the massacre of 100 of the children by his Imperial Guard.

On September 20, 1979, French paratroopers deposed him and reinstalled Dacko as president. Bokassa went into exile in France where he had chateaux and other property bought with loot he had embezzled. In his absence, he was tried and sentenced to death. Inexplicably, he returned to the Central African Republic in 1986 and was put on trial. In 1987, he was cleared of charges of cannibalism, but found guilty of the murder of schoolchildren and other crimes. The death sentence was later commuted to life in solitary confinement, but just six years later, in 1993, he was freed. He died in 1996.

Chronology

1921	Born February 22 at Bobangui, Oubangui-Chari, French Equatorial Africa.
1939	Joins French army.
1960	Becomes army commander in the newly independent Central African Republic.
1966	Stages coup and becomes president.
1977	Crowns himself emperor in a ceremony that practically bankrupts the country.
1979	Murders 100 schoolchildren; ousted by French troops.
1986	Returns to Central African Republic.
1987	Found guilty of murder.
1993	Freed.
1996	Dies November 3 in Bangui, capital of the Central African Republic.

Idi Amin

President
of Uganda
1924–2003

A member of the small Kakwa tribe, Idi Amin Dada Oumee joined the British Army in 1943. He was also heavyweight boxing champion of Uganda and a world-class rugby player.

A sergeant in the British Army, Idi Amin fought in Burma during World War II and in Kenya during the Mau-Mau revolt. When Uganda gained its independence in 1962, he became chief of the army and air force. In 1971 he staged a military coup, ousting President Milton Obote and making himself president. He promoted himself to field marshal in 1975 and became life president in 1976.

Mocked around the world for his pretension (he claimed to be victor over the British Empire, and a Scottish laird), behind the fancy uniforms he was a murderous thug. He killed his own wives and lovers if he suspected adultery. Larger tribes were persecuted and it is estimated that between 100,000 and 300,000 Ugandans were tortured and murdered during his reign.

In 1972 he expelled all Ugandans of Asian descent, leading to the collapse of the country's economy. He allied himself with Muammar Qaddafi in Libya and supported the Palestine Liberation Organization when it hijacked a French airliner carrying Jewish and Israeli passengers to Entebbe in July 1976.

In October 1978, Tanzanian troops, backed by Ugandan units who had fled over the border, invaded, reaching the capital Kampala on April 13, 1979. Amin fled to Libya, then settled in Saudia Arabia, where he lived in exile until his death in 2003.

Ex-British Army sergeant Idi Amin went on to promote himself a few more times.

Chronology

1924 or 1925	Born in Koboko, Uganda.
1943	Joins King's African Rifles.
1962	Becomes chief of army and air force after Ugandan independence.
1971	Ousts Milton Obote in coup; becomes president.
1972	Expels Ugandan Asians, crippling the economy.
1975	Promotes himself field marshal.
1976	Becomes life president; allows airliner hijacked by PLO to land at Entebbe.
1978	Ugandan nationalist troops backed by Tanzania invade.
1979	Amin flees Kampala April 13.
2003	Dies in exile in Saudi Arabia.

Robert Mugabe

Robert Mugabe trained as a teacher in a Catholic missionary school in Rhodesia. He was introduced to nationalist politics at university in South Africa and became a Marxist during time spent in Ghana.

President of Zimbabwe born 1924

On his return to Rhodesia in 1960, Mugabe helped form the Zimbabwe African National Union (ZANU) under Ndabaningi Sithole, a breakaway group from Joshua Nkomo's Zimbabwe People's Union run largely on tribal lines. In 1964, he was imprisoned for ten years for political activities and emerged from prison as ZANU's leader.

With Nkomo he headed the Patriotic Front (PF) while conducting a guerrilla war against Ian Smith's whites-only government from bases in neighboring countries. In 1979, he joined talks on majority rule in London. In elections the following year, ZANU won a landslide victory and Mugabe became prime minister.

Despite assurances, Mugabe turned Zimbabwe from a parliamentary democracy to a one-party socialist state with a central committee and a politburo. On December 31, 1987, he became the first executive president of Zimbabwe and first secretary of ZANU–PF. The white middle class began to leave and the economy faltered.

In 2000, to shore up his dwindling support, he began expropriating land owned by white farmers and giving it to "war veterans," who were usually too young to have fought in the war. Much of this land ended up in the hands of Mugabe's family and cohorts.

Since winning a largely discredited election in 2002, Mugabe's regime has been subject to U.S. and EU sanctions and political opposition, led by Morgan Tsvangirai, has intensified, despite intimidation tactics, which included the arrest and beating of Tsvangirai himself in 2007.

In 2008, Mugabe was narrowly defeated by Tsvangirai's Movement for Democratic Change in the first round of elections, but won the run-off election. However, in September of that year a power-sharing agreement was signed between ZANU-PF and the MDC, making Tsvangirai prime minister and Mugabe president. The agreement did little to quell the violence by ZANU-PF's henchmen. Zimbabwe remains a country struggling against repression and poverty.

Chronology

1924	Born February 21 Kutama, S. Rhodesia.
1963	Helps found ZANU.
1964	Jailed for "subversive speech."
1974	Stages coup to take over ZANU.
1975	Leaves jail and joins Patriotic Front to oust Ian Smith.
1979	Lancaster House talks in London.
1980	Elected prime minister of Zimbabwe.
1982	Ousts Nkomo from cabinet.
1984	Establishes one-party state.
1987	Becomes executive president.
1991	Introduces free-market reforms under pressure from the IMF.
2000	Gives white-owned farm lands to "war veterans," sparking violence.
2002	Re-elected president in fixed election.
2008	Power sharing agreement with MDC.
2010	Rumored to be dying of cancer.

Mugabe holds forth at a press conference, 1980.

Fidel Castro

**President
of Cuba
born 1926**

Although Cuba's revolutionary leader Fidel Castro honeymooned in the United States in 1948 and even considered staying on to study at Columbia University, in the 1960s he became America's most implacable enemy.

When Fidel Castro came to power in Cuba in 1959, he was not a Communist. Indeed, the United States did not hesitate to recognize his regime. He visited Washington, D.C, and assured congressmen that he would maintain Cuba's mutual defense treaty with the United States, and allow America to keep its naval base at Guantanamo Bay.

However, relations soon cooled when Castro began nationalizing American-owned sugar plantations. In February 1960, he signed a deal to sell sugar to the Soviet Union, a form of trade embargoed by the United States. In 1961 Castro's Cuban People's Party—called the Ortodoxos—merged with the Communist Party of Cuba and he became its general secretary. Castro then began fomenting revolution in Africa and Latin America and, in 1962, became a threat to the United States itself.

Castro was the illegitimate son of a sugar planter from Spain. He was brought up as a Roman Catholic, attending a Jesuit-run boarding school. During his five years at the University of Havana's Law School, he became involved in Cuba's violent brand of student politics. He was accused of the murder of another student leader, although the charge was never proved.

He participated in the attempted invasion of the Dominican Republic in 1947 and the riots in Bogotá, Colombia, the following year. In 1952, he stood as an Ortodoxos candidate for the Cuban House of Representatives. But the former president General Fulgencio Batista seized power and cancelled the elections.

On July 26, 1953, Castro staged an abortive insurrection in Santiago. His comrades were gunned down and he was arrested. At his trial, he attacked the repressive Batista government, concluding with the famous words: "History will absolve me."

On release in 1955, he went to Mexico where he formed the revolutionary organization called the 26th of July Movement. In December 1956, he returned to Cuba in a small motor cruiser called Granma. His small landing force was

Chronology

1926	Born August 13 near Birán, Cuba.
1948	Takes part in riots in Bogotá, Colombia.
1950	Joins the Cuban People's Party—the Ortodoxos.
1952	Becomes candidate for House of Representatives, but the elections are cancelled due to Batista's coup.
1953	Leads suicidal attack on barracks in Santiago de Cuba and is arrested.
1955	Released in an amnesty, flees to Mexico.
1956	Lands in Cuba with small band of guerrillas.
1959	Overthrows Batista government.
1960	Begins mass show trials.
1961	Repels CIA-backed invasion at Bay of Pigs.
1962	Cuban Missile Crisis.
1975	Sends troops to Angola.
1978	Sends troops to Ethiopia.
1980	Emerges as leader of nonaligned world, despite obvious Soviet backing.
1991	Collapse of Soviet Union forces Castro to open doors to tourism.
2008	Retires as president.
2011	Resigns as leader of Communist Party.

Hail, comrade! Castro with Soviet premier Nikita Kruschev on a visit to Moscow, 1964.

strafed by Cuban planes, and most of them were killed. Castro survived and, after three years fighting in the Sierra Maestra, rode to power at the head of a popular revolution.

Although Castro called for the United States to pledge $30 billion to make Latin America safe for democracy, he soon became authoritarian, first installing himself as Cuban premier, then president, then party chief, forcing the opposition into exile. Within months of taking power, he arrested some 4,500 anti-Castro suspects. They faced mass trials in 1960.

Under President Eisenhower, the CIA began to train anti-Castro Cuban exiles. Castro's response was to seize all U.S. assets in Cuba, including the American embassy. Although President Kennedy imposed an embargo on Cuban goods, many Europeans saw Castro as a romantic figure: Britain became the first nation to break the U.S. blockade.

United States' antipathy to Castro resulted in the unsuccessful invasion at the Bay of Pigs. Castro responded by allowing the Soviets to install nuclear missiles on the island, precipitating the Cuban Missile Crisis.

After the failure of the Bay of Pigs invasion, the CIA tried unsuccessfully to assassinate him and employed a "dirty tricks" division who dreamed up such ideas as poisoning his cigars and sprinkling depilatory powder in his diving mask. Castro had a well-known weakness for women. One of his lovers was a young German woman named Marita Lorenz, who lived in New York. After their affair was over, the CIA persuaded her to return to Havana to poison him. According to Marita, he knew she had come to kill him and handed her his revolver, but she could not pull the trigger.

At his trial, Castro attacked the repressive Batista government, concluding with the famous words: "History will absolve me."

Despite assassination attempts and international isolation—especially after the collapse of the Soviet Union—Castro clung on to power. Meanwhile his people risked almost anything to flee, and the country continued to decay. In 2003 seventy-five dissidents were jailed for up to twenty-eight years for daring to speak out against the regime. On the other hand, the Cuban people enjoyed a very efficient and generous welfare state and health system.

In July 2006 Castro temporarily handed power to his brother, Raul, before undergoing surgery. Two years later, he gave up the presidency permanently, and in 2011 he resigned as leader of the Communist Party, though he maintains his public profile via a newspaper column and occasional appearances on television.

Efrain Ríos Montt

**Dictator of
Guatemala
born 1926**

*The murderous dictator General Efrain Ríos Montt is, like many
of his Latin American peers, a product of the School of the
Americas run by the U.S. military in Panama.*

From the 1950s onward the notorious "coup school" taught its students
how to contribute to the defeat of Communism—and in so doing to further
U.S. interests—by usurping political power in Latin America by any
means necessary, including torture, assassination, and "disappearance."
Ríos Montt is also an ordained minister of the authoritarian, right-wing
Gospel Outreach evangelical Church, based in California, which has been
expanding fast in the South American region.

After a U.S.-orchestrated military coup in 1954, Guatemala became
a key component of the U.S. "counter-insurgency" strategy in Central
America. However, in 1960 a civil war broke out, which has continued
unabated ever since. The situation worsened in 1970 when the presidential
election was won by the "law and order" candidate Arana Osorio, who
promised to "pacify" the country by exterminating "habitual criminals"
and leftist guerrillas. In practice, this meant death squads linked to the
police or military began the organized murder of opposition leaders.

In 1974 Ríos Montt stood as leader of the progressive wing of the armed
forces. When it became clear that he had won the election, counting was
suspended and his opponent General Kjell Laugerud García was declared
the winner.

In March 1982, the elections were won by a coalition candidate,
General Angel Aríbal Guevara. But on March 23, a junta headed by
Ríos Montt seized power. He quickly dissolved the
junta and took absolute power, pledging to disband
the death squads, clean up corruption, and end the
guerrilla war by launching the so-called "guns and
beans" offensive against Guatemala's insurgents.
A subsequent report commissioned by the UN found
that at least 448 villages—mostly Indian—had been
wiped off the map. The targeting of the Mayan
peoples forced hundreds of thousands to flee to the
mountains or to neighboring Mexico. Many of those who remained were
corralled into "hamlets" to produce cash crops for export.

*"We do not have a policy
of scorched earth.
We have a policy of
scorched Communists."*

According to Amnesty International, in just four months there were
more than two thousand fully documented murders by the Guatemalan
army. However, U.S. President Ronald Reagan, who visited Guatemala at
the time, hailed Ríos Montt as "totally dedicated to democracy."

"We do not have a policy of scorched earth. We have a policy of
scorched Communists," Ríos Montt added.

Soon he became an international embarrassment. He was overthrown
in August 1983 by General Oscar Humberto Mejía Victores, who returned
the country to democracy. But this did not remove Ríos Montt from power

Chronology

1926	Born June 16 in Huehuetenango.
1950s	Attends "coup school" in Panama.
1974	Wins election but is denied presidency.
1982	Stages coup, begins genocide of Mayans.
1983	Ousted from office.
1998	Brother appointed to investigate "disappearances."
1999	Human rights case brought against him in Spain.
2003	Defeated in Presidential elections.
2006	International arrest warrant issued against him.
2007	Regains a seat in Congress and immunity from persecution.
2012	Placed under house arrest pending trial for genocide and crimes against humanity.

completely, far from it. The political party he founded, the ultra-right-wing Guatemalan Republican Alliance (FRG), expanded rapidly and gained control of a majority in Congress. The current President of Guatemala, Alfonso Portillo—a former guerrilla—is a Ríos Montt protégé.

Although Ríos Montt was actually president of the Congress, he was forbidden from running for president of the country by a constitutional law prohibiting former dictators from running for office.

However, he succeeded in getting the Supreme Court to overturn that ruling after inciting thousands of FRG supporters to cause havoc in Guatemala City, on a day that became known as "jueves negro" (black Thursday). The electorate, however, stood firm and he gained just 11 percent of the votes, well behind the victorious Óscar Berger of the Grand National Alliance.

Meanwhile, Ríos Montt's human rights record was threatening to come home to roost. His own brother, Bishop Mario Ríos Montt, who succeeded the assassinated Bishop Juan Gerardi as head of the Catholic Church's human rights office in Guatemala in 1998, promised to continue Gerardi's work, uncovering the truth behind the massacre of 200,000 people during the civil war and the genocide of the Mayan people during his brother's presidency in 1982–83.

His own brother promised to continue Gerardi's work, uncovering the truth behind the massacre.

In 1999, Nobel Peace Prize-winner Rigoberta Menchú brought a human rights case against Ríos Montt in Spain, as she felt it was impossible to bring him to justice in Guatamala. The campaign to prosecute Ríos Montt gathered momentum.

In 2006, a Spanish court issued an international arrest warrant, but Ríos Montt continued to seek political power at home. In 2007 he ran for Congress and won a seat, leading the FRG delegation once again and, more significantly, rendering him immune from prosecution.

However, in January 2012 Ríos Montt's term in office expired and he was brought before the Guatemalan court, where he was charged with genocide and crimes against humanity. He was placed under house arrest pending trial.

Pol Pot

**Leader of
Cambodia
1928–1998**

*Pol Pot was responsible for the deaths of more than a million
of his countrymen in a bloodthirsty experiment to create a
moneyless socialist society and turn the clock back in Cambodia
to "Year Zero."*

Born Saloth Sar, Pol Pot worked on a rubber plantation in his youth and
spent two years studying to become a Buddhist monk. During World
War II, he joined the resistance movement of Ho Chi Minh, which went
on to fight the colonialist French. By 1946, he was a member of the
underground Indochinese Communist Party. In 1949, he won a scholarship
to study radio electronics in Paris, but he spent his time there involved in
political activities, failing his exams three years in a row, a failure later
seen as contributing to his anti-intellectualism. Returning to Cambodia, he
worked as a geography teacher in a private school in the capital Phnom
Penh and wrote articles for left-wing publications.

When the French withdrew from Indochina in 1954, Prince Norodom
Sihanouk took power in Cambodia. Pol Pot opposed him. At the founding
congress of the Cambodian Communist Party in 1960, he was elected to the
central committee, becoming party secretary in 1963.

Fearing Sihanouk's repression, Pol Pot and other Communist leaders fled
to the jungle. There he took command of a guerrilla army dismissed by
Sihanouk as the Khmer Rouge—the Red Cambodians.

Although Sihanouk maintained a strict neutrality, the war in neighboring
Vietnam was destabilizing Cambodia. In 1970, the United States backed the
overthrow of Sihanouk's regime by the pro-American Genal Lon Nol. With
the backing of the Vietnamese Communists, who had established camps in
the border area, the Khmer Rouge waged a guerrilla war against Lon Nol.
The U.S. incursion into Cambodia in 1970 and its continuing cross-border
bombing campaign served to swell the Khmer Rouge's numbers and gain
international sympathy for its cause.

Chronology

1925	Born Saloth Sar January 25 in Kompong Thom province, Cambodia.
1946	Joins Cambodian Communist Party.
1954	Becomes a teacher.
1963	Flees the capital; takes to the jungle.
1975	Overthrows U.S.-backed government; declares Year Zero.
1979	Vietnam invasion ousts Khmer Rouge.
1982	Khmer Rouge joins coalition government.
1985	Retires.
1998	Dies April 15 in Cambodian jungle.

In 1975, as South Vietnam was falling to
the Communists, the Khmer Rouge overthrew
the U.S.-backed regime in Cambodia. Pol Pot
changed the country's name to Kampuchea. He
evacuated the capital Phnom Penh, marching
its two million inhabitants out into the
countryside at gunpoint. His aim was to convert
the educated middle-class city-dwellers into the
sort of virtuous hard-working peasants who had
supported his guerrilla army during its years
of struggle.

His plan was for Cambodia to revert back
to "Year Zero" and build a perfect socialist
society from the bottom up. Money and property
were abolished and books were burned. Private

houses were demolished, temples desecrated, and every possible symbol of Western technology—from cars to medical equipment—was destroyed.

Killing fields: skulls of Pol Pot's victims bear eloquent testimony to the brutality of the madman's reign.

To make his utopian society, Pol Pot transformed Cambodia into one vast slave-labor camp. Children were encouraged to inform on their parents and family life was all but extinguished. All professional people—including doctors and teachers—were killed, along with anyone who spoke French or wore glasses, which was considered the mark of an intellectual. Schools were closed, except for those devoted to political indoctrination, and everyone above the age of five was expected to work in the fields or factories sixteen hours a day. Those who could not meet production quotas or complained were killed on the spot. During the four years of Pol Pot's rule, around 1.7 million people—over 20 percent of the population—died as a result of disease, starvation, maltreatment, forced labor, torture, and execution.

During the four years of Pol Pot's rule, around 1.7 million people— over 20 percent of the population—died...

In 1979, the Vietnamese invaded and put an end to the holocaust. Pol Pot fled with his followers to the hill country on the Thai border where they continued the struggle with the backing of the United States', Chinese, and British governments. International condemnation and sanctions, led by a United States still embittered at the way the war in Vietnam had turned out, eventually forced the Vietnamese to withdraw and the Khmer Rouge returned to power in various coalition governments, while Pol Pot continued his murderous ways in the countryside. Eventually even the Communists disowned him, albeit half-heartedly. Pol Pot never stood trial for his many crimes, and he died of natural causes at the age of seventy.

Mobutu Sese Seko

Born Joseph-Désiré Mobutu, he joined the Belgian Congolese Army in 1949, rising to the rank of sergeant-major—the highest rank Africans could attain—before turning to journalism in 1956.

Mobutu joined the Congolese National Movement (MNC) in 1958, representing them at independence talks in Brussels. When the Congo won its independence in June 1960, he became defense secretary. Later that year he staged a coup and the popular leader Patrice Lumumba was killed.

In February 1961 he handed power back to President Joseph Kasavubu, staying on as commander in chief of the army, but in 1965 he staged another coup, this time taking the presidency himself. He ruled by decree and his party, the Movement for the Revolution, became the only party permitted.

He nationalized the copper mines in Katanga and Africanized names throughout the country. In October 1971, he changed the nation's name to the Republic of Zaire. The following January he took the name Mobutu Sese Seko Koko Ngbendu Wa Za Banga—which means "the all-powerful warrior who, because of his endurance and inflexible will to win, will go from conquest to conquest, leaving a wake of fire."

Re-elected president in 1970 and 1977, he looted the country, amassing one of the world's largest fortunes abroad. Inflation soared to 6,000 percent and the army was on the point of rebelling when he issued a five-million-zaire banknote (worth only $2) to pay them. Shopkeepers refused to take them, provoking the army to a killing spree resulting in three hundred deaths.

With the end of the Cold War, Mobutu lost Western support for his government, but he managed to hold on to power until, in 1997, friendless and ill, he was ousted by rebel leader Laurent Kabila and went into exile, first in Togo, then Morocco, where he died of prostate cancer.

Chronology

1930	Born October 14 in Lisala, Belgian Congo.
1949	Joins Belgian Congolese Army.
1956	Leaves army to become journalist.
1958	Joins Congolese National Movement.
1960	Represents MNC at independence talks; becomes defense secretary in new government; stages first coup.
1961	Returns power to president; stays on as commander in chief.
1965	Stages second coup; becomes president.
1971	Changes name of country to Zaire.
1972	Changes name to Mobutu Sese Seko Koko Ngbendu Wa Za Banga.
1993	Army on point of rebellion for not being paid; agrees to hold democratic elections but continues to stall.
1997	Ousted by Laurent Kabila; dies September 7 in Rabat, Morocco.

Mengistu Haile Mariam

An Ethiopian army officer, Mengistu was trained in the United States. Rising to the rank of major, he plotted a coup, deposing the Emperor Haile Selassie in September 1974.

Ruler of Ethiopia born 1937

Mengistu held Emperor Haile Selassie under house arrest in his palace until the following year, when he was strangled on Mengistu's orders.

On November 23, Mengistu ordered the assassination of the moderate chairman of the country's ruling Provisional Military Administrative Council (PMAC) and urged the killing of sixty leaders of the imperial regime.

In February 1977, now promoted to lieutenant colonel, Mengistu had the new chairman killed, making himself head of state. He then unleashed the "Red Terror" campaign to crush any resistance and, with Cuban soldiers and Soviet arms, he repelled the Somalian invasion of the Somali-speaking Ogden.

In 1984, he established the Ethopian Workers' Party. He drafted a new constitution and was elected president by a new national assembly. By this time Eritrea and Tigray in the north had rebelled. And when Soviet backing ended, he fled to Zimbabwe, where his fellow dictator Robert Mugabe still shelters him.

In January 2007 he was sentenced to life imprisonment in Ethiopia, having been found guilty in absentia of genocide. This sentence was amended to the death penalty following an unsuccessful appeal in 2008. However, the Zimbabwe government refuses to give him up.

Chronology

1937	Born in Kefa province, Ethiopia.
1974	Heads plot to overthrow the emperor; assassinates political rivals.
1975	Haile Selassie strangled on his orders.
1977	Murders other members of government; makes himself head of state; unleashes "Red Terror" campaign.
1986	Drafts new constitution.
1987	Elected president under its provisions.
1991	Flees to Zimbabwe.
2001	Given leave to stay permanently.
2007	Found guilty of genocide.

Mengistu (left) and his advisers during a parade in Addis Ababa, 1975.

Saddam Hussein

*The fifth president of Iraq, Saddam Hussein was a cruel and
ruthless dictator whose violent suppression of the people who
opposed him eventually led to his execution in December 2006.*

*Saddam Hussein
at the Iraqi Special
Tribunal in 2004.*

Born Saddam At-Tikriti and orphaned at nine, he was raised by his uncle
Khairallah Talfah, who led an unsuccessful Nazi-backed coup in 1941.
A slow learner, Saddam was refused entry into the Baghdad Military
Academy. Instead he joined the Baath Socialist Party in 1957.

Having already killed a Communist politician who had stood against his
uncle, Saddam volunteered to assassinate President Adbul Karim Kassim
who had overthrown the Iraqi monarchy in 1958. The attempt failed and
Saddam, wounded in the leg, fled to Egypt, dropping the name At-Tikriti and
using his father's first name, Hussein,
as his last to avoid arrest.

He returned to Baghdad, where he
organized the Baathist militia, who
seized power in 1963. Later that year,
the Baathists were ousted and Saddam
was imprisoned, but he escaped and,
as leader of the Baathist party, staged
another coup in 1968. At first he
ruled jointly with President Ahmad
Hassam al-Bakr, who stood aside in
1979. Saddam then consolidated his
position as head of state by putting to
death hundreds of rivals.

Saddam and his family took hold of
all the levers of power. He instigated
a cult of personality in an effort to
make himself leader of the Arab
world and, using his secret police,
eliminated any opposition. Asked by
a European interviewer about reports
that the Baghdad authorities might
have tortured and killed opponents
of the regime, Saddam replied: "Of
course, what do you expect if they
oppose the regime?"

In 1980, he invaded the Iranian
oilfields, but the offensive bogged down
into a costly war of attrition, ending
with a stalemate in 1988. Hundreds of
thousands had been killed. That same
year, he used nerve gas against the
Kurds who opposed his rule.

Chronology

1937	Born April 28 in Tikrit, Iraq.
1957	Joins Baath Party.
1960	Makes unsuccessful assassination attempt on Iraqi president; escapes to Egypt.
1962–63	Studies at Cairo Law School.
1963	Leads Baath militia in coup; ousted from power and imprisoned.
1968	New coup brings Baathists and Saddam back to power.
1979	Takes over as president; murders hundreds of rivals.
1980	Invades Iran.
1988	Gases the Kurds.
1990	Invades Kuwait.
1991	Kicked out of Kuwait; drains the homeland of the Marsh Arabs.
2003	Ousted from power by Anglo-American invasion. Captured hiding in a hole by U.S. troops on December 14.
2006	Found guilty of crimes against humanity and executed on December 30.

In 1990, he invaded Kuwait. The following year a U.S.-led coalition drove his forces out of Kuwait, inflicting a crushing defeat but leaving him in power. During the war, Saddam authorized missile attacks on Israel, a noncombatant. His forces terrorized the populace of Kuwait and, while withdrawing, polluted the Persian Gulf with oil spills and set fire to over three hundred oil wells. Putting down a resulting rebellion of Shiia in the south of Iraq, he razed towns and drained their marshland home.

Twelve years of United Nations sanctions failed to remove him from power and in 2003 Anglo-American forces invaded Iraq, believing that Saddam had weapons of mass destruction, although no such weapons were found. Saddam disappeared, but his two sons Uday and Qusay, both psychopathic killers, died in a gun battle. Mass graves soon came to light: Saddam's executioners were still killing hundreds of enemies of the regime, even as American tanks rolled into Baghdad.

On December 15, 2003, soldiers from the U.S. 4th Infantry Division, acting on intelligence received over the eight months since they had been in the country, mounted a dawn attack on a small Iraqi town named Ad-Dawr. The town is located approximately ten miles south of Saddam's home town of Tikrit. During the raid, they discovered an underground bunker. Crouched in the bunker, dishevelled, unshaven, and unwashed, was the former dictator. Saddam chose surrender without a fight.

Tried by the Iraqi Special Tribunal for the 1982 murder of 148 Shiites in Dujail, he was found guilty of crimes against humanity and sentenced to hang. Footage of him being led to his death on December 30, 2006 was broadcast around the world.

"Politics is when you say you are going to do one thing while intending to do another. Then you do neither what you said nor what you intended."

Saddam Hussein

Slobodan Milosevic

President
of Serbia
1941–2006

Slobodan Milosevic plunged his people into war and his ruthless pursuit of "ethnic cleansing" led to numerous massacres, until finally NATO intervened to defend the people of Kosovo.

Slobodan Milosevic was the Serbian leader during the break-up of Yugoslavia. He was responsible for a bloody and ruthless war that resulted in the ethnic cleansing of Kosovan Serbs, forcing NATO to send military aid to stop the slaughter. Milosevic was eventually overthrown by his own people and handed over to the UN War Crimes Tribunal in The Hague.

Milosevic was an obscure Communist Party apparatchik until April 1987, when he made a speech in Pristina, capital of Kosovo, to a crowd of angry Serbs protesting against alleged harassment by the majority Albanian community. He famously said that no one would ever be allowed to beat them, a statement of defiance that became a rallying cry for Serb nationalists.

He wrested control of the Serbian Communist Party from his friend and ally Ivan Stambolic and, in 1989, he became President of Serbia. The following January the Yugoslav Communist Party fell apart when the Slovenian and Croatian delegations walked out of the party congress in Belgrade, leading to the break-up of the party.

More than three years of war followed, the bloodiest in Europe since World War II.

In July, the Serbian Communist Party changed its name to the Serbian Socialist Party, but it retained its assets, power structures, and control of the state media. Milosevic warned that if the Yugoslav nation dissolved, it would be necessary to redraw Serbia's boundaries to include Serbs living in other republics.

When Croatia declared independence, the Serb minority who had proclaimed regional autonomy in Krajina looked to Milosevic for support—and got it. By December 1991, the army and Serbian separatists had taken nearly a third of Croatia's territory, including Krajina and most of eastern and western Slavonia. Some twenty thousand people were killed, and a further 400,000 made homeless. The UN imposed economic sanctions.

Bosnia declared independence in April 1992 and violence broke out throughout the republic, with Milosevic vowing to defend the Serbian minority there as well as protecting them from what he called "Croatian genocide" and "Islamic fundamentalism." More than three years of war followed, the bloodiest in Europe since World War II. Serbian war crimes, including, shamefully, massacres within the so-called UN safe areas of Gorazde and Srebrenica, came to public attention and Serbia was further isolated as a pariah state.

In 1995, Croatia recovered much of the territory earlier captured by the Serbs, resulting in the exodus of some 200,000 Serbs from their self-proclaimed Republic of Serbian Krajina. This was followed by a successful offensive against Bosnian Serbs in Bosnia. Three weeks of NATO bombing forced Milosevic to the bargaining table and the Dayton Peace Agreement ended the war in Bosnia.

The war had made Milosevic unpopular, but he rode out massive waves of protests against his government during the winter of 1996–97, when tens of thousands of people took to the streets, contesting the results of municipal elections. Many demonstrators were brutally beaten by the Serbian police. After three months of protests, Milosevic caved in, conceding stolen municipal elections to the opposition. But in July 1997 Milosevic was elected president of Yugoslavia by the lame-duck federal parliament, which was controlled by his supporters.

He then tried to drive the Muslim majority out of Kosovo. NATO began its bombing campaign, and there was a feeling of disbelief among many Yugoslavs. But Milosevic rode out the storm, and for a while consolidated support as Serbs united against the West.

The NATO bombing campaign left Serbia in ruins. Milosevic finally withdrew his troops from Kosovo. With Serbia's infrastructure ruined and its economy crippled by new sanctions, Milosevic remodeled himself as the rebuilder of the nation. However, in 2000 he was forced to call elections.

When Milosevic refused to recognize the election victory of opposition leader Vojislav Kostunica, hundreds of thousands of people took to the streets and a national strike was declared. The Serbian Orthodox Church and parts of the state media withdrew their support. Ten days after the election, protesters stormed parliament and the state TV station, setting them alight. Many police officers took off their helmets and joined the protesters.

On October 6, Milosevic was forced to concede defeat. The following day Kostunica was sworn in as the new Yugoslav president. In June 2001 Milosevic was handed over to The Hague tribunal for trial, but died of a heart attack in March 2006, before the trial ended.

Chronology

1941	Born August 29 in Pozarevac, Yugoslavia.
1963	Joins Yugoslav Communist Party.
1987	Speech in Pristina brings him to national attention.
1988	Installs followers in power in autonomous provinces, including Kosovo.
1989	Ousts Ivan Stambolic to take over as President of Serbia.
1990	Alters constitution to take direct power of autonomous provinces.
1991	Backs Serbians in fighting in Croatia, taking almost a third of Croatia; Serb leaders in Bosnia proclaim separate state.
1992	War breaks out in Bosnia.
1995	Croatian forces recover Serb-held territory; 200,000 Serbs flee; NATO air strikes force Milosevic to accept Dayton Peace Agreement.
1996	Anti-Milosevic protests brutally suppressed.
1997	Becomes Yugoslav president.
1998	Milosevic rejects calls for end to ethnic cleansing in Kosovo.
1999	NATO planes bomb Serbia; Serbs withdraw from Kosovo.
2000	Vojislav Kostunica wins election; strikes and civil disobedience force Milosevic to step down.
2001	Sent by the Serbian government to The Hague to face trial.
2002	Trial begins.
2006	Dies of a heart attack.

Hissen Habré

Dictator of
Chad
born 1942

Thousands of murders and human rights abuses have been attributed to Hissen Habré's one-party regime, causing Habré to be dubbed "the African Pinochet."

Born in 1942 in the Boukou district of Chad, Hissen Habré was educated in Paris. He returned to Chad in 1971, but left for Tripoli in Libya the following year where he established a guerrilla army called the Armed Forces of the North (FAN). In 1978 Habré was appointed prime minister, succeeding Félix Malloum, but it was a position he held for just a year.

Moving across the border into northern Chad, Habré's army funded itself by extortion and ransoming kidnapped Europeans. In 1980, President Goukouni Oueddei requested the support of neighboring Libya in the continuing struggle between the Christian/black southern region and the Arab/Muslim north, forcing Habré to withdraw to the Sudan. However, he soon reoccupied towns in eastern Chad.

When the peacekeeping forces of the Organization of African Unity withdrew in 1982, Habré seized power, but an opposition government under Goukouni Oueddei was formed with Libyan backing. A full-scale civil war broke out in 1983, which Habré won with French backing. When France withdrew its troops in 1984, Libya pushed deeper into Chad in 1986. With French and U.S. support—both countries wished to curb Libyan attempts to extend its power in the region—Habré pushed the forces of Muammar Qaddafi out of the country and began to make incursions into Libya.

Hissen Habré, leader of the rebel FAN army, in 1975.

Chronology

1942	Born in Boukou, Chad.
1971	Returns to Chad after education in France.
1971	Forms guerrilla army in Tripoli.
1980	Forced to withdraw to the Sudan due to Libyan intervention.
1982	Seizes power.
1983–84	Civil war breaks out; Habré wins with French backing.
1986	Libya invades northern Chad; Habré ousts Libyans with French and U.S. support.
1987	Truce called.
1989	Foils coup.
1990	Ousted by Idriss Déby; flees to Senegal.
1991	Commission accuses Habré of 40,000 murders and 200,000 cases of torture.
2003	Extradition proceedings begin.
2008	Sentenced to death in absentia by a Chadian court.
2011	Senegal officials announce Habré's extradition to Chad but it is subsequently halted.

A truce was called in 1987, but in April 1989 Habré faced an unsuccessful coup attempt by the interior minister, Brahim Mahamot Itno, with military advisers Hassan Djamouss and Idriss Déby. Itno was arrested and Djamouss was killed, but Déby escaped and began new attacks the following year. By late 1990 his Movement for Chadian National Salvation forces had captured Abéché in eastern Chad, and on December 1 Habré fled to Cameroon, then to Senegal, where he remains to this day, nominally under house arrest in Dakar. Déby formed a new government with himself as president.

A commission set up in 1991 accused Habré's administration of 40,000 political murders and 200,000 cases of torture.

Habré stands accused of countless atrocities and murders during his time in power, including genocide against several of Chad's ethnic groups. A commission set up in 1991 accused Habré's administration of 40,000 political murders and 200,000 cases of torture. Human rights groups say they have detailed ninety-seven cases of political killings, 142 cases of torture, and 100 "disappearances." The United Nations backed his prosecution for human rights violations, but Senegal has repeatedly blocked attempts to extradite him, or to try him in Senegal. The African Union urged Senegal to put an end to the years of wrangling and negotiation and either put Habré on trial or send him to a country that would do so.

The campaign to bring Habré to justice continues.

Muammar Qaddafi

**President
of Libya
1942–2011**

*Born a Bedouin in the desert, Muammar Qaddafi was reared in
the tradition of fighting imperialism. His grandfather had been
killed by an Italian colonist in 1911. However, he showed no
gratitude to the British who expelled the Italians from his native
Libya in World War II: to Qaddafi, all Europeans were alike.*

From an early age Qaddafi idolized Gamal Abdel Nasser, the Egyptian
soldier who seized power in Egypt in a coup in 1954 and nationalized the
Suez Canal. As a child, he would tune into Radio Cairo and, at the age
of sixteen, Qaddafi began his own revolutionary cell, which plotted the
overthrow of King Idris of Libya even though the king had turned his back
on his former allies, the British, and joined the Arab League.

In 1959, oil was discovered in Libya, which brought wealth to
the country, but also brought more foreigners in the shape of the oil
companies. At the University of Libya, Qaddafi read history and political
science. Initially he was a Marxist, but then rejected Communism in favor
of Islam. At university he became known as a troublemaker for his fierce
condemnation of Israel and Zionism.

Realizing that Nasser had come to power via the army, Qaddafi
enrolled in the Libyan Military Academy in Benghazi when he graduated

Chronology

1942	Born near Surt, Libya.
1964	Enrols in Military Academy.
1965	Graduates and is sent to signals school in England.
1966	Commissioned as a signals officer.
1969	Deposes King Idris I and takes power; ousts co-conspirators with help of Egyptian troops.
1970	Closes British and U.S. bases; expels Jews and Italians.
1973	Nationalizes oil companies.
1974	Espouses "Islamic socialism."
1976	Publishes part one of *The Green Book*.
1980	Publishes part two of *The Green Book*.
1986	U.S. bombs Libya in retaliation for Qaddafi's support of terrorism.
1988	Liberalizes economic policies after his ideological doctrines are seen to fail.
1988	Libya accused of bombing of Pan Am Flight 103: U.S.-inspired sanctions put in place.
2003	Libya admits responsibility for Pan Am bomb, and agrees compensation for the victims.
2011	Ousted from power and killed during the Libyan civil war.

Qaddafi attends the 12th African Union Summit in Addis Ababa, Ethiopia, February 2009.

from university in 1964, and here he and his friends continued to plot the overthrow of the Libyan government.

After he graduated from the academy in 1965, he spent a year in England at signals school. He also studied armored warfare there. On his return he was promoted Adjutant of the Signals Corps.

In 1969, Qaddafi and his young friends pre-empted senior officers who were plotting against the king and staged a bloodless coup of their own. They seized the Royal Palace, government offices, the radio and TV stations, and the newspapers. Qaddafi was just twenty-seven years old.

However, some of the conspirators wanted to maintain ties with the West, so Qaddafi asked Nasser for help. With the aid of Nasser's troops, Qaddafi made sure that his anti-Western line prevailed. British and American bases were closed and, in 1970, Jews and Italians were expelled.

Qaddafi tried to implement Nasser's brand of socialism, nationalizing the oil companies and starting rapid industrialization. However, this plan failed. He also tried to export revolution and was implicated in attempted

Muammar Qaddafi

The remains of Pan Am Flight 103 lie forlornly outside the Scottish town of Lockerbie, 1988.

coups in the Sudan and Egypt, and he interfered in the long-running civil war in Chad.

Banning alcohol and gambling in accordance with Islamic principles, he began a cult of personality and outlined his vision of Islamic socialism in two volumes of *The Green Book*, published in 1976 and 1980. His regime backed a number of revolutionary or terrorist groups including the Provisional IRA in Northern Ireland, the Black Panthers and the Nation of Islam in the United States, and Carlos "the Jackal." Émigré opponents were assassinated by his agents, who also backed terrorist outrages in Europe perpetrated by Palestinian or other Arab extremists.

He is thought to have financed the Black September Movement, responsible for the kidnapping of Israeli athletes at the 1972 Munich Olympics, and the bombing of a German discotheque in 1986, which killed one American and one German and wounded 150, including forty-four Americans. In retaliation, U.S. warplanes based in the UK bombed Libya in 1986, killing or wounding several of his children and narrowly missing Qaddafi himself.

When Pan Am Flight 103 was blown up over the Scottish town of Lockerbie in 1988, suspicion eventually fell on Gadaffi's Libya, and in 2001 a Libyan government official was found guilty of the bombing. Libya admitted responsibility in 2003, and agreed a compensation package to be paid to relatives of the victims.

In February 2011, the Arab Spring uprisings in Tunisia and Egypt spread into Libya, triggering a civil war in which Gadaffi showed no regard for the welfare of his people. The International Criminal Court issued an arrest warrant against him for crimes against humanity and, though he was eventually captured alive after the fall of his last stronghold, Sirte, in October, he was killed by fighters from the Libyan National Liberation Army before he could come to trial.

Samuel Doe

The twenty-first president of Liberia, Samuel Doe was the first to be of native African descent, as opposed to Americo-Liberian. He held office from 1986 until his assassination in 1990.

**Dictator
of Liberia
1951–1990**

Born in Liberia in 1951, Samuel Doe enlisted in the army at the age of eighteen. Trained by U.S. Special Forces, he rose to become a master sergeant by 1979.

Like many indigenous Liberians, Doe resented the privileges garnered by the descendants of the freed American slaves who had founded the colony in 1822. On April 12, 1980, Doe and seventeen other soldiers staged a pre-dawn attack on the presidential mansion in the capital, Monrovia, killing President William R. Tolbert and thirty other government officials.

Seizing control of the government, Doe promoted himself to general and commander-in-chief. Heading the People's Redemption Council, he suspended Liberia's 133-year-old constitution and had thirteen of the former president's associates summarily executed. Members of his own Krahn tribe took over all the important positions.

Following an attempted coup, Doe held elections in 1985. Despite accusations of vote-rigging and intimidation, a special election committee determined that he had won 51 percent of the vote. On November 12, Doe survived another coup attempt. In retaliation, the army went on the rampage. Reports of human rights violations soared and there were charges that millions of dollars of U.S. aid had been "mismanaged."

Doe's repressive regime shut down newspapers, banned political activity, and cruelly mistreated several of the country's ethnic groups. By 1989, the country was in a state of civil war. In July 1990, rebel forces advanced into Monrovia and their leader Charles Taylor demanded Doe's resignation. He refused and peace negotiations were conducted by the United States and the Liberian Council of Churches. Five African nations sent troops to keep the peace, but the attempt did not succeed. After being wounded in a gunfight, Doe was captured and died under torture soon after.

Charles Taylor took power and presided over a period of strife until his resignation in 2003. The election of Ellen Johnson Sirleaf in 2005 marked a turning point in the history of this ravaged nation.

Chronology

1951	Born May 5 in Tuzon, Liberia.
1969	Joins the army.
1980	As master sergeant, stages coup.
1980–85	Brutally suppresses opposition and installs his own tribe in top jobs.
1985	Rigs election.
1985–89	Allows army to loot the country.
1989	Civil war breaks out.
1990	Refuses to resign; captured and tortured to death September 9/10.

Glossary

auto-da-fe The public ceremony at which the judges of the Spanish Inquisition declared the sentences of heretics. This was followed by the imposition of sentences by secular authorities, which usually meant burning at the stake.

Aztec calendar The calendar system used by the Aztecs, who lived in Mexico from the 14th to the 16th century CE. The Aztecs used two calendars, the 365-day civil cycle and the 260-day ritual cycle.

boyar A member of the highest rank of Russian aristocracy, from the 10th to the 17th century.

communism A political theory originating with Karl Marx, according to which property and resources should be communally owned, and wealth should be distributed according to people's needs. In practice, communist states have been characterized by government ownership of resources, rather than communal ownership.

coup d'état The sudden and illegal overthrow of a government by force. The original, French meaning of the phrase is "blow to the state."

cult of personality The concentration of power in a single charismatic leader. The term is often used to refer to totalitarian states, where the leader is praised and idolized by the state media.

daimyo A powerful lord in Japan, often ruling vast tracts of land, from the 10th to the 19th century.

demagogue A political leader who exploits the prejudices and emotions of his or her audience rather than making factually accurate arguments.

ethnic cleansing A policy enacted by one religious or ethnic group to remove the population of another group from an area, making the area homogeneous. The policy often involves murder, torture, forcible deportation, and destruction of property.

fascism A political movement characterized by authoritarianism and a belief in the supremacy of one national or racial group above others. The term "fascism" was originally applied to Mussolini's Italy (1922–43), but has since been used more broadly.

Germinal A spring month in the French Revolutionary Calendar.

Gregorian calendar The form of calendar used by most of the world today. It was introduced in 1582 by Pope Gregory XIII to ensure the date matched the seasons.

guerrilla warfare A form of warfare in which a small group of combatants, including armed civilians, takes on a larger, conventional army. It is characterized by the use of ambushes, sabotage, and tactics favoring speed and surprise.

Inquisition, the A system of religious courts created by Pope Gregory IX (circa 1232) to discover and persecute those holding heretical (which is to say, non-mainstream Christian) beliefs. The Inquisition was most active in France and Italy and was notorious for its use of torture.

Jacobin A member of the Jacobin Club, an organization formed in the wake of the French Revolution, which argued in favor of egalitarianism but endorsed extreme and violent tactics.

Julian calendar The calendar which was introduced by Julius Caesar in 46 BCE. In it, a year was 365 days long with a leap year every fourth year. As a year is slightly shorter than 365.25 days, the Julian calendar gained approximately a day a century. It was replaced in 1582.

junta A government controlled by military leaders who have taken power by force.

kabaka The title of the king of Buganda.

martial law The rule by the military instead of by civilian government. Martial law is often declared in an emergency and it generally leads to a suspension of civil rights. In theory, martial law is temporary, but in practice it can last indefinitely.

Messidor A summer month in the French Revolutionary Calendar.

naphtha A volatile and highly flammable hydrocarbon liquid.

plebiscite A vote in which the entire electorate is asked to accept or reject a particular proposal. It is often used as a vote on the choice of ruler.

procurator An official of the Roman Empire.

senate A council possessing supreme legislative powers. Most senates consider the legislation proposed by a lower house.

tetrarch The Roman title for the ruler of part of a region or province. Regions were usually split into four parts, with a tetrarch to rule over each part.

Thermidor The eleventh month of the French Republican Calendar`.

tribune The title of an official in Ancient Rome. The role of tribunes was to protect ordinary citizens from the sometimes arbitrary actions of magistrates.

tribute The payment that one state gives to another in acknowledgment of its submission.

trireme A boat with three rows of oars on each side, used in Ancient Greece and Rome.

yaws An infectious tropical disease.

For Further Reading

Arnold, James R. *Saddam Hussein's Iraq*. Minneapolis, MN: Twenty-First Century Books, 2008.

Gay, Kathlyn. *Mao Zedong's China*. Minneapolis, MN: Twenty-First Century Books, 2007.

Hook, Sue Vander. *Adolf Hitler: German Dictator* Minneapolis, MN: Abdo Publishing Company, 2011.

Marcovitz, Hal. *Dictatorships (Exploring World Governments)* Minneapolis, MN: Essential Library, 2011.

Price, Sean. *Ivan the Terrible: Tsar of Death*. New York, NY: Children's Press, 2008.

Web Sites

Due to the changing nature of Internet links, Rosen Publishing has developed an online list of Web sites related to the subject of this book. This site is updated regularly. Please use this link to access the list:

http://www.rosenlinks.com/gph/tyran

Index

126

Acknowledgments

Picture Credits

All images © Hulton Getty Images Ltd, except for page 86 (Shutterstock), page 102 (Online Communism Photo Collection, photo Z260) and pages 114 and page 121 (Wikimedia).